Way of Holy Joy

Selected Writings of Sofia Cavalletti

Selected, translated, and
introduced by Patricia Coulter

Catechesis of
the Good Shepherd
Publications

Nihil Obstat
Very Reverend Daniel A. Smilanic, JCD
Vicar for Canonical Services
Archdiocese of Chicago
November 25, 2011

Imprimatur
Reverend Monsignor John F. Canary, STL, DMIN
Vicar General
Archdiocese of Chicago
November 25, 2011

The *Nihil Obstat* and *Imprimatur* are declarations that the material is free from doctrinal or moral error, and thus is granted permission to publish in accordance with c. 827. No legal responsibility is assumed by the grant of this permission. No implication is contained herein that those who have granted the *Nihil Obstat* and *Imprimatur* agree with the content, opinions, or statements expressed.

Text © 2012 Catechesis of the Good Shepherd. All rights reserved.

Catechesis of the Good Shepherd Publications is an imprint of Liturgy Training Publications (LTP). Further information about these publications is available from LTP or Catechesis of the Good Shepherd, PO Box 1084, Oak Park IL, 60304; 708-524-1210, fax 708-386-8032. Requests for all other aspects of the Catechesis should be directed to this address.

WAY OF HOLY JOY: SELECTED WRITINGS OF SOFIA CAVALLETTI © Archdiocese of Chicago: Liturgy Training Publications, 3949 South Racine Avenue, Chicago, IL 60609; 1-800-933-1800, fax 1-800-933-7094, e-mail orders@ltp.org. All rights reserved. See our website at www.LTP.org.

Cover photos by Douglas R. Gilbert © 2003.

Printed in the United States of America.

Library of Congress Control Number: 2012931989

ISBN 978-1-61671-052-1

WHJ

Contents

Translator's Acknowledgments   iv

Introduction   v

1. Baptism: Foundation of Peace   1
2. The Child as Parable   10
3. The Child and Peace   21
4. An Adventure: The Catechesis of the Good Shepherd   29
5. My Readings   60
6. Curriculum Vitae   79

About the Author   82

Translator's Acknowledgments

As much as it is desired, it is simply not possible to thank all those who helped these writings of Sofia to come into book form; only a few can be named here:

Dr. Silvana Montanaro, Mrs. Augusta Poluzzi, and the Cocchini family for their generous hospitality across the years, especially during those joyful weeks in 2003.

Cardinal Aloysius Ambrozic (+2011) and Archbishop Marcel Gervais for their support of this catechesis from its very first years in Canada.

William Targett, director of the Office of Formation for Discipleship, Toronto diocese, for providing the time and practical means necessary to do this work; and Lesley Critton and Connie Price for their technical assistance.

Members of the Association of the Good Shepherd Catechesis in Canada, and in the United States, particularly Mary Mirrione, the Board, and the Formation and Publications Committees; and the team of the *Journal of the Good Shepherd Catechesis.*

The Liturgy Training Publications staff, particularly Margaret Brennan, our editor and collaborator.

Rebekah Rojcewicz for her collaboration in translating Sofia's and Gianna's writings over many years; Brother Ignatius Feaver, OFM CAP, for his accompaniment of this catechesis since its beginning in Toronto.

All our beloved family and friends who have companioned us with their love and prayer.

Introduction

Why these writings? First, I would like to offer something of the story as to how they came to be included in this little book, then a word about the title, and finally, an expression of appreciation for Sofia.

In September 2003, an opportunity opened to spend time with Sofia in Rome. Surprisingly, this time together was completely unstructured and for about three weeks we met almost daily. The conversations roamed freely, without any agenda. Sofia touched on many themes, among which—not surprisingly—there were two constants: the God-child relationship, and her near half-century of "passionate" work, as Sofia describes it in these pages, in service of that relationship.

In the course of those weeks, Sofia gave me copies of some of her writings on these themes, which have not been translated into English to my knowledge. Several of these essays are collected here, and I have added another one previously published in English (chapter 2). This compilation, spanning over 40 years, is arranged in chronological order, except for Sofia's *curriculum vitae,* which is placed at the end.

Sofia notes that she wrote this "for the Multicultural (International) Montessori Congress, October 3, 1996, Rome." One of the two variations of this curriculum, the sketchier one, contained this brief addendum: "Sofia Cavalletti, biblical scholar, has published various books and articles on the following subjects: Hebrew (scripture, studies), Judaism, and religious education. In 1954, she began the Catechesis of the Good Shepherd with Gianna Gobbi."

In this two-sentence summary of her life up to that point, her naming of Gianna stands out. Because the Good Shepherd Catechesis is a motif woven through most of these chapters, this collection of Sofia's writing would not be complete without an explicit mention of Gianna Gobbi.

Gianna's unfailing commitment to this catechesis lasted over 50 years, right up to her death. For those wishing to know more about Gianna's contribution, there is her wonderful book, *Listening to God with Children: The Montessori Method Applied to the Catechesis of Children*. Sofia wrote in her Introduction to it: "It will be of interest to anyone who seriously approaches the child and considers the child in his or her spiritual potential" (pp. x–xi).

Indeed, the importance of Gianna's presence and contribution to the Good Shepherd Catechesis can hardly be overemphasized, although it is interesting to note that neither Gianna nor Sofia ever ascribed to themselves the role of "founders." I think Sofia speaks for them both in her reference here to Gianna, at the beginning of the catechesis in 1954; she states simply that they were "collaborators."

This fact recalls another that has caused me to wonder over the years: that this catechesis was without an identifying name until around its 30-year mark, and when it was named, it was not by Sofia or Gianna. The name of "the Good Shepherd Catechesis" was given by someone else; and it was received by them in the same way they received the catechesis, as a gift.

Both of these facts are small, to be sure, yet they are significant in that they seem, to me, to point out their shared singleness of focus: on the Giver. And perhaps this could be ascribed to humility, that "cardinal virtue" which Sofia synthesizes in this quote of Saint John of the Cross in chapter 4: "Your eyes in mine aglow/printed their living image in my own."

A word about the title: before Sofia died in August 2011, she was able to give her "yes" to the final draft as a whole and to review some of these chapters word for word. But the book was left untitled. I then chose the title, based on this passage in chapter 4:

> Young children seem to want to point out to us that *their* way of going to God is different, for example, from what is indicated in the *Imitation of Christ*. This is a book that, even though it originated in the medieval period, has been used to educate many generations up to recent times. This book speaks about the 'royal Way of the holy Cross' as the privileged path for going to God, whereas the child seems to wish to point out to us the 'royal Way of holy Joy.'

The words "joy" and "way" are foundational. You will discover that joy is a recurring theme in these pages; perhaps it could be called Sofia's theme song.

The word "way" has levels of meaning here. It conveys the concrete image of a path or pathway that the children opened to her and led her along, both in terms of her whole life's work and also her journey with God. I believe this is why she names the child as "master-teacher."

Certainly Sofia is writing about the child in the chronological sense of that word, but she is also addressing the evangelical dimension of being a *child,* and the Gospel sayings of Jesus with respect to "becoming" like a child. In so far as this invitation of Jesus is addressed personally to each of us, because we are all begotten of God, these writings provide valuable insights into our own identity and true nature. That is to say, the child's way of being in relationship with God, which Sofia explores here, is ours as well. For instance, that whole-person way of living the covenant relationship with God ("My body is happy," a child prays); that joy and depth, intimacy and enjoyment, which the child experiences in the presence of God—these are also our precious patrimony as children of God.

My hope is that this little book will encourage us all to venture forward confidently along this way of holy joy.

As this book has become Sofia Cavalletti's posthumous work, it seems fitting to conclude with some words of a personal nature.

Sofia frequently referred to Psalm 21:4, when writing in response to the death of someone. Often, she would change the pronoun to fit the person about whom she was writing. And since this work is dedicated both to Sofia (+August 2011) and Gianna Gobbi (+January 2002), I will adopt her usage:

> They asked you for life; you gave it to them—length of days forever and ever. (Psalm 21:4)

Now that Sofia and Gianna have entered this life eternal, the following sentence from Saint Paul speaks to the deep emotion of my heart and those of many persons, children and adults alike, around the world:

> How can we thank God enough for you in return for all the joy that we feel before our God because of you? (1 Thessalonians 3:9)

Finally, in closing, it is important that the last words come from Sofia herself. On March 14, 1993, she wrote the following few lines, which she wished to be read at her funeral.

> I wish to remind those who will be participating at my funeral rites, that a funeral is a celebration of the resurrection, a profession of faith in life—in the force of life, in life's being stronger than death.
>
> The Christian faith—it could be said—is an obstinate faith; each time it is confronted by death, it proclaims that death does not have the last word. And this is what we believe, what we affirm, and what we want to announce to the world, because we know that there has already been a first victory of life over death: in the Resurrection of Jesus Christ.

Patricia Coulter
18 October 2011

Chapter One

Baptism: Foundation of Peace

Translator's Note:
This chapter was originally published in *Via, Verità e Vita: Rivista Catechistica* 30 (November–December 1970). Sofia is writing this a few years after the Second Vatican Council, during which the Rite of Baptism was renewed. In this context, it is interesting that her Center of Catechesis—underway for 15 years or so by the time of this writing—had already been introducing children to the meaning of the Rite of Baptism by means of the "signs," which the Council was just now bringing back into clearer relief.

    This essay gives an early indication of the importance Sofia attaches to giving children, including those from the youngest age, direct access to the "sources," namely the Bible and, in this case, the liturgy. It also provides an early glimpse into the experiential thrust of this catechesis; in the examples she describes here, that hallmark emerges. The foundation of this journey of catechesis is rooted in actual experience with children, which Sofia lived continuously, even into her 90s.

    This essay also affords an early reflection on the child as an agent for peace; this theme recurs in chapter 3, written 25 years later. Here, one notices how Sofia's scholarship in the Hebrew language is brought to bear so fruitfully in her examination of the word *peace*. This, however, represents definite challenges with regards to translation. In addition, Sofia's knowledge of many languages, ancient and modern, means that she writes with great precision, and even coins words at times.

    Therefore, I would like to look at two terms she uses repeatedly, *shalom* and *shallem*, in the hope that these words will not be a stumbling block, but rather will enhance the essay's meditative richness for the reader.

    In this essay Sofia takes the time to develop the significance of the root connection between the Hebrew words *shalom*, meaning "peace," and the less familiar word, *shallem*. At the risk of using an unfamiliar word, I have kept as close as possible to its English equivalent, "integrality," which the dictionary defines as "lacking nothing essential," and have used it interchangeably with the word "wholeness."

Similarly, Sofia speaks of the child's heart as *integro,* meaning integral, complete, whole, entire; here the words "integral" and "whole" have been used. In short, the term *shallem* connotes wholeness and integrality, and also suggests other meanings associated with the word: the quality of integrity; being integrated; the integration of one's whole being.

Finally, about the format: I have taken the liberty of inserting the subheadings into most of these essays. This is the only essay that previously contained subheadings, which appear to have been added by the original editor, and have been retained here.

Education for peace is not a specific task of religious formation, but of education in general. "To avoid conflicts is the work of politics," Maria Montessori wrote, "to build peace is the work of education." We would like to add that perhaps it is the only true task of education, because, in our opinion, to educate for peace is to help the person to realize oneself "integrally." It is significant that, in the Hebrew language, concepts of "peace" and "integrality" are linked to the same root, thus evidencing the profound connection between "integrality, wholeness" and "peace." A person cannot give oneself peace, harmony, if there is no unity within oneself, if there is no absence of ruptures and divisions in the person.

Thus the first place in which "wholeness" needs to exist, so that there will be peace, is in the heart of the human person. If the heart of the person is not *shallem,* integral, whole, that person will not be able to give oneself *shalom,* peace.

The expressions of fellowship which abound in our time surely represent building blocks on the path of peace, on the condition, however, that the existence of divisions in the human heart are not allowed to continue. Although the human heart might burn with love for the oppressed, if it still is seething with hate for the oppressors, that person would not yet be "integral, whole" and would not yet be able to build the foundation for peace.

Baptism: Foundation of Peace

Replica of the baptismal font Sofia commissioned for the atrium.
Photo by Carolyne-Marie Petch.

Furthermore, even a fellowship that embraced all humankind, but only humankind, would not yet represent *shalom,* peace, because it would exclude the most important part of reality: God. The human heart that does not open itself to the religious reality would remain equally split, mutilated, would not yet be *shallem.*

This is the reason why I want to affirm that an education for peace cannot be given, unless it is within a religious perspective. And I would like to add that the most suitable subject of, the most fecund group for, an education for peace are children, because their hearts are still "integral."

The Child: Suitable Subject for the Education to Peace

The heart of the child is "integral, whole," because the child lives the relationship with God spontaneously and naturally, in a bond that is intimate and steadfast, profound and essential. The God-child relationship is so strong that it is even resistant to negative environments: generally, a child who lives in an atheistic environment is particularly sensitive to the religious reality and avid for it.

I can say this based both on the experience of persons who are dedicated to the observation of children's needs in an intelligent manner and also from my own experience, even if it is partial. I think I can affirm the existence of a discrepancy between the psychological construction of the child, and the child's way of living the religious reality.

Because of the first, the child takes everything from the environment, whereas young children manage to defend their relationship with God, even when there is nothing in the environment that helps them in this regard. Clearly, therefore, the source of this relationship is not in the environment—by environment I mean the persons and all the other elements that comprise it—but rather in a mysterious gift that unites together Creator and the human creature, the child who has come forth intact from God's hands.

The person who does not wish to follow us in this affirmation will need to renounce the investigation into the origin of the relationship, full of ease and spontaneity, of the child with God; all the same, however, that person will not be able to deny its evident existence.

Therefore the child's heart is "integral" in the sense, we would say, of its vertical dimension. But is the child "integral" in the horizontal dimension as well? Are there ruptures in the child's heart, in the sense that the child discriminates between those to be loved and those not to be loved?

I fear that the reader will find it harder to accept my positive response to this question than it was to reject what I said about the previous point. And yet we all have often witnessed the truly edifying sight of children who are capable of reaching out and embracing someone who shortly before had been fighting with them, or lost patience with them, or had treated them badly. We have all seen the sight of the child who is incapable of rancor, who accepts even the violent friend with the same love.

It is sad to see how the immense potentialites of love within children too often end up being thrown back on the children and withdrawn into themselves, because they do not find an adequate and wise response from the people in the world around them. In our opinion, it is not exact to speak about the "potentialities of love" in children, because we are dealing with a reality that is already present and operative within them, which naturally moves toward realization in later developmental planes in adolescence and mature adulthood.

Who will save that richness of "integral" love, which God has placed in the child? We said that an education for peace cannot preclude God; now we wish to be more precise and say that it cannot preclude Christ, because the fullness of unity has already been realized in Christ. The cross, sign of Christ's Death and Resurrection, symbolizes this: its uppermost part touches heaven and its lower part penetrates to the depths of the earth; in a single gesture it extends to the farthest reaches—east and west—embracing all the people of the world.

The power of Christ penetrates everywhere and to everyone, because Christ has gathered all things, all places, and all people into his love; for this reason he is called "our peace," the universal point of convergence, in whom the harmony between heaven and earth and among all peoples is being realized.

During the baptismal rite, the sign of Christ's cross is made on the forehead of the person as a sign of one's vital insertion in Christ, of one's assimilation into Christ "our peace."

The child lives the values of unity, peace, and harmony both naturally and supernaturally; but the child lives these values at a level which is not yet conscious or deliberate. The life of the human person consists in transforming the gifts that are offered into gifts that are accepted and desired and lived with ever more awareness. The work of education must be directed to helping children become conscious of these gifts, so that they can make them the building material of their very person.

Helping Children Know the Gift of Baptism

The child who is living out his or her Baptism needs to know its richness; the new Rite of Baptism offers signs that are so obvious and, I would say, tangible, that catechesis has no need to invent anything in order to present it to children.

The Sign of Light

Saint Paul speaks explicitly of Baptism as an "illumination" and the baptized as "illumined." The new baptismal rite[1] prescribed that the lighted candle, which is consigned to the baptized person as sign of the new life being received, be lighted from the paschal candle.

It is the first baptismal sign that we present to children, and it already lets us "see" the vertical and horizontal dimensions of that life which, in Christ, unites us to the Father and to our brothers and sisters. Children readily recognize that their own candles would stay unlit had they not been lighted from that paschal candle, which is the sign of the risen Christ. The light given to us is God's gift and we can receive it in ourselves because, in the first place, Christ's light has overcome the darkness.

And yet the light from the large paschal candle is slowly diffused throughout time, increasing the number of persons who are joined to and illumined by it, right up to the present day with these children who now, with awe in their eyes, are contemplating their lighted candles.

They "contemplate" it in the true sense of the word, because by means of the candle's light they see the invisible; in this regard, it is striking to observe that children usually do not speak about light but about "goodness," and "the life of Jesus," almost as though they are not really seeing the material element of the lighted candle.

The vertical dimension of the "light" is integrated with the horizontal vision. That is to say, the relationship that is established is not only between God and the individual creature: that same light the children contemplate in the candle they hold in their hands is also the same light that burns in the candle of their companion, and in the candles of all the children, each of whom has also gone to the paschal candle and taken from it the light that enflamed their own candle.

The same reality of life is in all of us; we are linked together by the presence of the life of the risen Christ in us.

One child had worked on a drawing of the Good Shepherd and sheep. Some time later, after the presentation of Baptism, the child returned to the drawing and added a lighted paschal candle beside the sheep: "Because," he explained, "we all have the light of Christ inside; we are all sheep of his fold."

The Sign of the Good Shepherd

Indeed the Good Shepherd parable is another "sign," and one of even greater value, in helping children to become aware of the "integrality" of the relationship that Baptism creates in them. With this sign, the theme of light is made explicit in the key of love. There is one unique shepherd, who cares for and protects those sheep that have been born, through Baptism, into the sheepfold; the Good Shepherd who knows each of them by name in a mutual exchange of love: "I know my sheep and my sheep know me."

The shepherd's love is a richness that enriches all the sheep of the fold, in a relationship that unites them to Christ and one another. This is the point that children of three to four years of age grasp in the parable of the found sheep (Luke 15:3–7), which integrates with the Johannine parable (John 10:1–18).

The moral problem in the parable of the found sheep is not felt by children of this age in any way, and the whole problem of mercy and forgiveness cannot be addressed with them (and it is absolutely useless to try to approach it). In spite of this fact, this parable can be presented to young children just the same. Young children will greet the return of the sheep with expressions of joy, because this is how the bond of love not only reintegrates with the shepherd, but also unites the sheep together as well. The sheep that had strayed away had interrupted that thread of love linking it with the shepherd and all the other sheep; the return of the sheep re-establishes that bond of love.

The Sign of the Vine

This same reality is presented to children who are a little older (around the age of First Communion) through the allegory/parable of the True Vine (John 15). In this parable there is a fusion of the themes of life (light) and love. Baptism is what gives us birth as a bud on the True Vine; from that moment a vital relationship is established between the newly-baptized and the Father and with one's brothers and sisters, who "remain" united in the Vine. "As the Father has loved me, so I have loved you; remain in my love" (v. 9).

The Father's love, concretized in the person of Christ, comes to the individual person; the person responds with love to the Father, always through the person of Christ, concretizing that love in one's actions. As one part of the plant cannot exist in a relationship that excludes the other branches, so too the same "life-giving sap," the life of the risen Christ, flows within each baptized person. Therefore, all the baptized find themselves united to the Father and to all one's brothers and sisters in an intimate, life-giving relationship.

The harmony and peace between the Father and his creatures and among people themselves—that harmony of which Christ is the source, and therefore Baptism—is such an essential good that Baptism is presented as life. To damage that harmony and that "integral" peace, to which all persons are called, becomes an offense against life itself, a "disintegration" of oneself.

With respect to the theme of peace, offering catechesis by means of signs, whether liturgical signs or parables, shows itself as the best way to help children—and also adults—become more aware of these gifts they have received, and which they are called to live with an adherence of the will that grows ever deeper and more conscious.

Once again, offering catechesis by means of signs shows itself as the best way, not only because it renders the supersensible reality materially concrete, but also because it is the nature of the sign to present this reality not so much for the purpose of "putting it in front of our eyes" as an object of contemplation, but for the purpose of helping us to enter into this reality "as protagonists."[2]

Endnotes

1. Translator's note: As noted, Sofia is writing this only a few years after the Second Vatican Council (1962–1965), during which there was a renewal of the Rite of Baptism.

2. S. Marsili, *"Segni sacri: storia e presenza," Il Segno Nella Liturgia* (Padova: CAL, 1970), 8.

Chapter Two

The Child as Parable

Translator's Note:

This article first appeared in *Euntes Docete XXV* (Urbaniana Pontifical University) in 1972 and is a seminal study on many accounts. It is an invitation into a firsthand, in-depth immersion into a primary "source": Sacred Scripture. As such, it offers a unique penetration into the Gospel vision of the child according to Jesus. The uniqueness of this reflection is due partly to Sofia's particular preparation, along three lines.

One is Sofia's training in philology, which entails a delving into the wealth of words, with an exactness that enables her to uncover deeper levels of meaning. Another is her long experience as translator of the Hebrew and Christian Scriptures; thus she conveys the importance of and respect for every word—above all for the "Word" (her capitalization)—in these evangelical texts relating to the child. A third element Sofia brings to her interpretation of these Gospel passages is her lengthy and, in her estimation, invaluable apprenticeship with Eugenio Zolli in studying the Judaic approach to the Bible (which she addresses in chapter 5).

In that same chapter, Sofia identifies this approach as the midrashic method of interpreting the Bible. My understanding of what she writes here about the way of *midrash* is that there is not only a whole world within each sacred word of Scripture, but a new world also emerges when similar words are connected to one another.

Thus in this chapter, which pores over the words of Jesus about the child, we are given a window through which to catch flashes of that hidden force (as in the "mustard seed") which creates the inexpressible bond between Jesus and the child. Even more, it is like a door that offers entry into an exploration of the Christian mystery itself, especially as embodied in the child, whom Jesus presents to us as a living parable, according to Sofia's insight.

The Child as Parable

Sofia's atrium in Rome. A representation of a material for the parable of the True Vine; on the wall is a print of an ancient statue of the Good Shepherd from the catacombs in Rome. Photo by Carolyne-Marie Petch.

My original translation of this essay first appeared in the *North American Montessori Teacher's Association Quarterly*, 7 (Fall 1981), 43–47.

Many works have been written about the importance attributed to the little child in various evangelical texts, and after Simon Legasse's masterful book[1] on the subject, there seems little left to add. Nonetheless, if we are to consider the child in the Gospel as a "human parable," as Legasse maintains,[2] the very nature of the parable is to remain always open to new interpretations, revealing ever greater riches. It is for this reason that we allow ourselves to offer some observations in relation to the little child in the Gospel.

Two Series of Gospel Texts

The Gospel presents two series of texts that surround the little child. The first series includes the following passages: Matthew 19:13–15; Mark 10:13–16; and Luke 18:15–17. These texts are partially synoptic. All three have in common the passage in which Jesus tells his apostles to let the children come to him, without hindering them. Mark and Luke add the statement on the need to receive the Kingdom of God like a little child in order to enter into it, thus manifesting the exemplarity of the young child.

The second series of texts includes: Matthew 18:1–6; Mark 9:33–37; and Luke 9:46–48. At the outset we note that in all three Gospels this series of texts follows the miracle of the healing of a possessed boy, which, according to Luke 9:43, aroused the admiration of the crowd. This miracle, in its turn, is immediately followed by the foretelling of the Passion and Resurrection.

These are hard words, which the disciples prefer to ignore. Only Matthew inserts the episode of the Temple tax (17:24–27) between these two texts and the passage relating to children. Whereas in Mark and Luke, the miracle, the foretelling of the Passion, and the text referring to children follow in direct succession.

In the second series of texts we find once again the theme of welcoming the child, but it is transformed. These passages do not speak any longer about the little child as the model for entering the Kingdom of God.

Rather, they say that to receive the little child is the same as welcoming Christ, and whoever welcomes Christ welcomes the One who sent him. Nevertheless, the principal subject of the passage seems to be the response that was called forth by the disciples' question: Who is the greatest (μείζων) in the Kingdom of God?

Who Is the Greatest in the Kingdom?

In the Gospel of Matthew, Jesus responds to this question by calling a "little child" (παιδίον), and exhorts the apostles to convert and "become like little children" (τά παιδία) in order to enter the Kingdom, and to become "little" (ταπεινόω) so as to be the greatest (μείζων). The text of Matthew is the least altered, according to Legasse.

In the Gospel of Mark, the disciples do not dare to reply to Jesus when he questions them as to what they had been speaking about, because they were asking themselves who was the greatest (μείζων). Then Jesus says that the one who wants to be first (πρωτος) must be last and the servant of all (έσχατος και πάντων διάκονος); the appearance of the little child introduces the theme of welcoming.

In the Gospel of Luke, Jesus reads the unvoiced question in the hearts of the disciples about the "greatest" (μείζων), takes a "little child" (παιδίον) and affirms that it the littlest (μικρότερος) who is great (μέγας).

We find a contrast in all these responses of Jesus, expressed in various forms:

little/great

first/last

    servant

great/the one who makes oneself little.

In this contrast, the two opposite poles are found to be present in children, for it is precisely because they are the littlest that constitutes them as great.

Sofia's window, with the mustard seed plant in the foreground and the clock tower in the background. Photo by Sofia Cavalletti.

The Theme of Contrast
In the Gospels

The theme of contrast, a frequent theme in the New Testament, has abundant precedents in the Old Testament. In the teaching of Jesus, this theme often takes the parabolic form, for example, the parable of the mustard seed that is the smallest (μικρότερος) of all the seeds and becomes the greatest (μείζων) of shrubs (Matthew 13:31–2).

We also find this theme, intermingled with other points, in various parables: the parable of the yeast, which leavens the whole dough (Matthew 13:33); the parable of the growing seed, which gives the full grain in the ear (Mark 4:29); the parable of the seed, which brings forth grain, some a hundredfold, some sixty, some thirty (Matthew 13:8).

In each of these parables, however, the little/great contrast is different from what is said in relation to the little child. The seed *is* the smallest, and it *will be* the greatest of shrubs. The seed is a potentiality which will be realized in a second or later moment in the tree; between the seed and tree, and between the yeast and the dough, the relationship is diachronic. Whereas, in the child, the relationship between the little/great is synchronic; the child *is* the greatest, precisely because the child *is* the littlest.

There is no need to wait in order to see the greatness within the child to be realized at a later time; the greatness is already present in the child's littleness. There is no need to look far into the future to grasp the child's greatness, as in the case of the mustard seed. It is necessary, however, to be attentive to the greatness in the present littleness, to know how to see the power, already present and active, within it. If it were justifiable to make a distinction among the virtues which express the foundational religious attitude in its three different aspects, we could say that the mustard seed is an object of hope, the little child is an object of faith.

Therefore, to shed some light on the passages relating to the child, it will be necessary to refer to other New Testament passages where this theme of contrast is found, and in which this contrast is synchronic.

In the Letters of Saint Paul

One text that seems to us to meet these requisites is from Saint Paul's Second Letter to the Corinthians: "[P]ower is made perfect in weakness" (2 Corinthians 12:9). Paul is juxtaposing two elements which appear irreconcilable, no less than the little/great contrast. He expresses a contrast that seems untenable; yet the two terms are united synchronically in one single realization. It is Saint Paul who arrives at an apodictic enunciation of this principle, which is threaded through both the Old and the New Testaments; he is the one who has experienced the power of God at work in his weakness (2 Corinthians 12:10); he is the one who knows himself to be an earthen vessel that holds a treasure (2 Corinthians 4:7).

Paul's words arise from his own situation; however, they are not tied to that specific situation, but to the apostle himself. These words emerge from a situation which Paul has suffered personally and through which he comes to enter into a law of the Christian life itself that is universally valid. That is, Paul intuits a theme in its profundity and reaches the point of being able to formulate it in an essential form; it is the theme that constitutes a basic motif, and perhaps *the* foundational motif, throughout all of Scripture.

The whole of biblical history could be found to be recapitulated in Paul's succinct expression: from the time when Abraham, already old and weak, becomes father and progenitor of descendants as numerous as the stars in the sky; from the time when an enslaved and fugitive people encounters God in the desert; and most of all, from the time when, in the ultimate weakness of the death of his Christ, God accomplishes the greatest deed of his power.

We could say that the words of Paul are the programmatic enunciation of the paradox of Christianity.

The Child in Context

If the approach we are proposing is valid, the passage relating to the little child would thereby acquire another dimension, and that little child, whose littleness and weakness are signs of greatness and strength, would appear to us as bearer of an astounding reality.

To understand better what is said with respect to the child, it seems necessary to consider the context in which the passage occurs, so as to include the two texts which precede it: Jesus' foretelling of his Passion and the miracle of healing.

In our estimation, these two episodes and the passage about the child are not casually situated, one randomly following the other. Rather, they are linked together by a single thread and form one unified whole. Legasse observes that the discourse about "the greatest" shows the incapacity of the Twelve to enter into the mystery of redemptive humiliation.[3] This is the same incapacity, if we may be allowed to add, that the apostles demonstrated in not accepting the announcement of the Passion: "But they did not understand this saying; its meaning was concealed from them, so they could not perceive it" (Luke 9:45).

The miracle stirred great enthusiasm in the crowd. On other occasions like this Jesus corrected the crowd's enthusiasm so that they would not let themselves be deceived with respect to his real nature as Messiah. Jesus is the Messiah who must suffer and die in order to rise; he is also a Messiah who is powerful and victorious, and a Messiah whose power is realized through a paradox—by means of the utmost weakness, death.

In the presence of a paradox such as this, however, the apostles' ears remained closed; they did not manage to accept it. And then, seeing that his words had been insufficient, facing the extreme importance of what he wanted to teach and the extreme difficulty in receiving it, Jesus adds a living example of what he wanted to proclaim: the child, in whose weakness and littleness is the greatest.

Jesus sees the disciples' difficulty, tries to make his teaching more concrete and striking, and shows them a person in whom his words were in some way rendered visible and tangible. That is, Jesus returns to his customary teaching method: the parable. But this time he turns to a "human parable" (Legasse). If the truth contained in parables is generally concretized in an image expressed in words, which the hearer grasps by means of listening, in this instance the truth is embodied in a visible image: that child whom Jesus takes in his arms and puts among the apostles. It is the child, in its littleness, who is the greatest; and the little child is the greatest precisely because of its littleness, for it is weakness such as this that the power of God needs in some way in order to be realized.

The Master corrects and addresses the crowd's enthusiasm at his miracle in two ways:

1) with his foretelling of the Passion, which will precede the Resurrection;

2) with the parable of the child, who incarnates in itself the fundamental law of Christianity.

Christ and Children

In our estimation, the words of Christ do not have any moralizing intent. But they do intend to point out in the "little child" an existential type, in whom the paradox of the coexistence of littleness/greatness, powerlessness/power, is manifested in a particular way—that paradox which Christ will live to the utmost in his Death and Resurrection.

This, therefore, explains the identification of welcoming the "little child" with welcoming Christ, which is the theme that concludes this passage in all three synoptics: "Whoever welcomes this child in my name welcomes me, and whoever welcomes me welcomes the one who sent me" (Luke 9:48). Such an identification means that in the little child, as in Christ, it is evident that the power of God is manifested in weakness.

This also explains why the Kingdom of God belongs to children in particular, and why they can be the model for the one who wants to enter the Kingdom. Between Christ and children there exists a profound affinity, which does not depend upon the possession or practice of this or that moral virtue, but rather on the existential situation of the child: the child is the privileged bearer of that reality which Christ has come to reveal and to realize in its complete fullness in his person.

That preference of Christ for children, which so many speak about, springs forth from a certain kind of "blood relationship" or kinship which exists between them. To prevent little children from going to Christ is to hinder like going toward like.

The Child—A Parable

If the child is a parable, then, as with every parable, the child is composed of two elements: one is visible and obvious; the other element is mysterious, which must be made the object of an ever-deepening search. These elements, however, are inseparable, just as a chemical compound cannot be separated (Nicolas-Théodore de Saussure) without becoming some other thing.[4] It is the same with the child: we cannot separate the littleness from the greatness in the child, without losing sight of what the child is and the reality of which the child is the sign.

If, as it has been noted, it is easy to perceive the obvious element in the parables, staying on the superficial level, it is not as simple to enter into the mysterious reality of which this element is the bearer. If, as it is said of parables in general: "Let anyone with ears listen!" (Matthew 11:15), it can be said of the child-parable: "Let anyone with eyes see!" It is easy to see that the child is little and weak; it is not as easy to see a power within the little child, not in potential but present.

As we mentioned, the penetration into the meaning signified by the visible element in the parable is always open to greater insights and constantly new discoveries. For some persons, the divine power present in the child's weakness may be manifested in that particular rapport that unites the child to God in a life-giving relationship, which has all the strength and spontaneity of a basic fact of life. For others, it may be manifested in the richness and essentiality of the child's prayer.

Yet it is the very nature of the parable to resound in a different way within each person who listens to it—or, as in this instance, to each person who sees it. We do not wish to impose any personal interpretation on the child-parable. We have only wanted to point out the parabolic character of the child, so as to offer an invitation to look at the child with eyes that know how to see beyond appearances.

Endnotes

1. Simon Legasse, *Jésus e l'enfant,* Paris: J. Gabalda, 1969.
2. *Ibid.,* p. 193.

3. *Ibid.,* p. 19.

4. It can be assumed that Sofia is referring here to the pioneering work of the Swiss scientist Nicolas-Théodore de Saussure (1767–1845). His research in isolating definite chemical compounds was groundbreaking, such as, for example, his study "Chemical Research on Plant Matter."

Chapter Three

The Child and Peace

Translator's Note:
At the center of Sofia's penetrating work here is a photograph that appeared on the cover page of the periodical *Lettera dalla Collina* (12 June 1995), a periodical of the community of Nevè Shalom/Wāhat al–Salām in Israel, a land Sofia visited many times. Written at the top of the cover page is the origin of the name of this village, taken from the Book of Isaiah 32:18: "My people will abide in a Nevè Shalom" (oasis of peace). This village in Israel is the springboard for Sofia's thoughts on the child and peace.

The chapter threads around this tender image of two very young children, one Israeli, the other Arab, kissing. There is, however, nothing sentimental in the thoughts evoked in Sofia by this tender sight. Instead, it provokes her to probe the "sad" contrast between what is captured in the photo and what all too often remains captive within children: their rich potentialities of love and thus for peace.

Sofia asks difficult questions: "Who will save this richness that God has placed in the child?" She also asserts, in the building of and educating for peace, the necessity of a religious perspective and, more precisely, the need for Christ "our peace."

We all agree in reading this title that it expresses a desire which we all have at heart, but which we see, with great regret, is very far from being realized. If we were to read the title as an indication of a present reality, it would easily be said that we are living in a dream or in a utopia.

Nonetheless, we have before our eyes a photograph from the cover of the June 1995 issue of the review *Lettera dalla Collina*. We see two little children, one a few months old and the other around two years of age who are kissing tenderly, and the note underneath the photograph informs us that one of these children is Palestinian, the other Israeli.[1]

We are not in utopia: we are in the land that is burned by sun and war, where the birds no longer sing. It is exactly in this place that something came to birth which opens the heart to hope. Indeed, if we think of peace as something that is truly rooted in the human spirit, it needs to begin with a kiss like the one the photo shows us.

We are in Nevè Shalom/Wāhat al-Salām, the place born of Father Bruno Hussar's dream.[2] It is very rare for a "dreamer" like him to know how to harmonize within himself openness to a vision that seems unrealizable with the capacity to translate it into reality. Here, in fact, one does not talk about peace; one lives peace.

As those familiar with this place know, the foundations of the village are the nursery for the littlest ones and the school, with its *Dumiah* space (*Dumiah* in Hebrew means "silence"), an area consecrated to that "silence" which is "praise" to the One God, who "hears prayers" (Psalm 65:2).[3]

Two great potentialities for peace are found in Nevè Shalom/Wāhat al-Salām: the interreligious dialogue (it would be more exact to say the dialogue among spiritualities) and the child.

In our estimation, we are not dealing with two different potentialities, but rather with two potentialities which, in the child, become one.

Our foremost wish here is to speak about the child. This village's sense of reality has led them to a firm belief: in order to build peace, it is necessary to begin with the littlest children.

Since the time of the Gospels, when Jesus said that children, more than any others, have the right of citizenship to the Kingdom of God, and when children were presented to us as models to imitate so as to be part of that Kingdom, speaking about the child's particular religious capacities is not something new.

Nevertheless, conclusions are often reached that are in complete opposition to the Gospel: it is said that the child has a religious life only if it is similar to the adult's, that is, only if the rational and volitional elements are prevalent in it; the contrary case, in the opinion of many, is that there is no religious capacity in the young child.

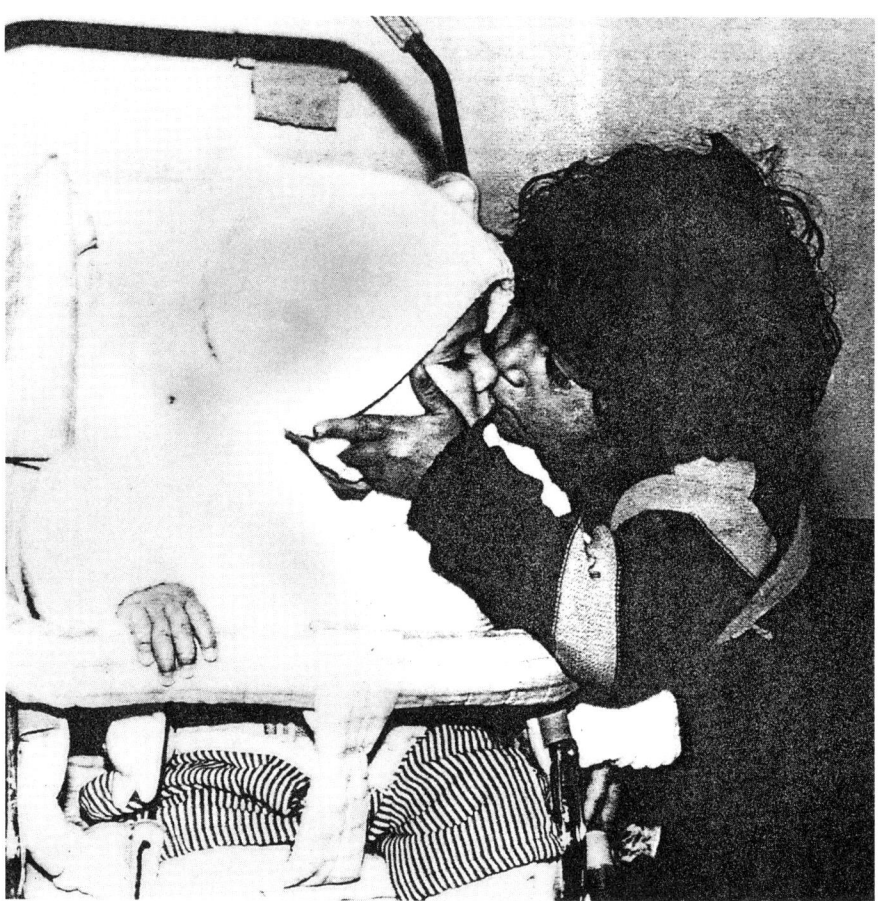

"In the nursery: A little Jewish girl and a little Arab girl. Peace begins here." Used with permission.

If we pass from the religious field to the realm of peace, a statement like this would be very discouraging. What possibility would there be for an adult, who was born into and has grown up in a certain culture of war, to educate someone in a real way for peace? At Nevè Shalom/Wāhat al-Salām they speak, quite rightly, of a school *for* peace and not a school *of* peace, because there is a clear recognition that no one feels capable of teaching in such a school.

No one, with the exception of the child.

Why do we say this?

We can say this because, from observing children from the religious point of view, we have been able to see the capacity within the child to be truly a *master-teacher*.

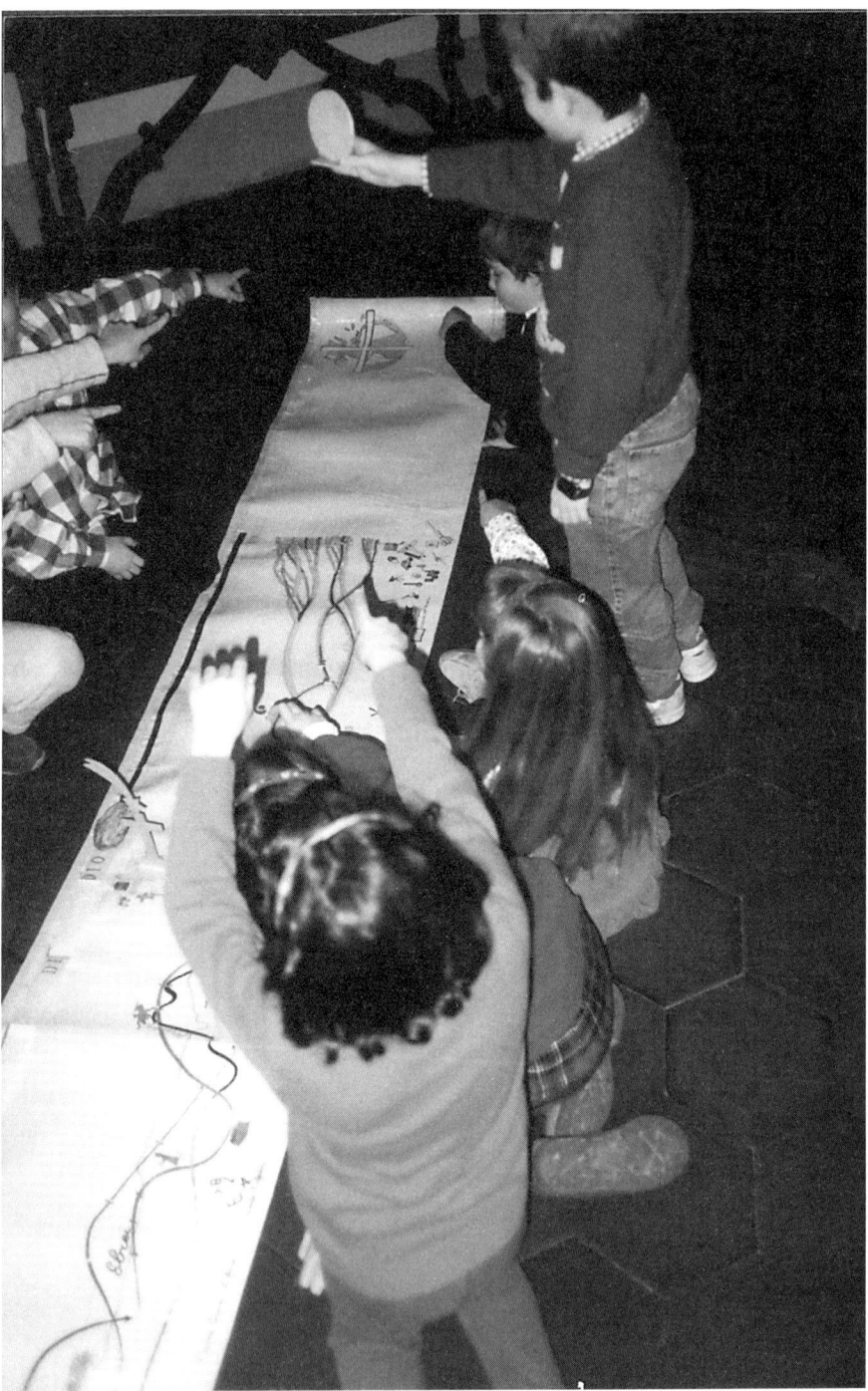

The timeline on the theme of the History of the Kingdom of God.
Photo by Sofia Cavalletti.

From a religious perspective, many things observed in young children lead us to say that they live their relationship with God in a way different from that of adults. Many adults say that they have found God in the trials of their lives, in moments of solitude and abandonment, in pain and suffering. The child finds God in joy and experiences a profound joy in the relationship with God. It is a different joy from what children live in many other experiences, which often leave them tired, tense, and enervated.

The joy that children experience in the relationship with God puts them at peace, a deep peace, which lingers within and which they do not wish to leave. It is a peace that makes one think that a deep chord has been touched within them and that they want to continue to listen to its lingering vibrations. It is a recollected joy and it spreads. It leads one to think that the child has found in the relationship with God the satisfaction of a vital, existential need.

The child finds God in fullness, not in indigence. For the child, God is not "a stop-gap God," to use Bonhoeffer's expression. This Lutheran theologian, killed by the Nazis, searched for God "at the center of life." God, he says, "wants to be recognized in life and not only when death comes; in health and vigor, and not only in suffering; in our activities, and not only in sin."[4]

Bonhoeffer speaks about a way of finding God, not by contrast (we are poor, God is rich; we are suffering, God is impassible; we are radically powerless, God is omnipotent, etc.), but by likeness.

We have seen in the child's relationship with God what appears to be a mutual attraction by means of a likeness. The child seems to find in God that richness of love that is found in himself or herself, even if it is limited. The child searches for a pole of attraction that can correspond with that love within himself or herself. And when it is found, the child immerses himself or herself in it with a deep enjoyment and with feelings of total satisfaction. The child goes to God in joy and recognizes God in joy.

If this is true—as we think it to be true (and we say this based on some 50 years' experience with children, beginning at the age of two, and in very diverse countries and environments)—it seems sufficient reason to affirm that the interior structure of the child presents itself as *different* from what is manifested in other stages of life. It is precisely this difference that should awaken the adult's interest and spur the adult to observe the child attentively, so as to place oneself, according to the word of the Gospel, in the school of the child.

At this point I would like to return to the photo of the kiss between the little Palestinian and the little Israeli. What is peace for these two children? Is it an external element about which they must be educated? Or is it rather a way of being, which is only waiting for the environment in which they are living not to impede them in realizing it? Is there in the child a "connaturality" with peace—the peace that is *shalom,* namely, harmony, integrity—as there is a "connaturality" with God, who is the fullness and source of *shalom*?

Is making children live in a situation of dissension and war something that makes them "live badly," as happens with adults? Or rather, does the situation block the full realization of their deepest nature, with all the consequences that this can carry? The many people on the waiting list of Nevè Shalom/Wāhat al-Salām seem to be in agreement with this last point, because all of them have asked to enter the village "for the sake of their children."

Maria Montessori writes: "If the era in the history of human evolution that is characterized by the constant outbreak of war can be called the 'adult period,' then the period in which we will begin to build peace will be the 'age of the child.'"[5]

We think the "age of the child" will be realized if we, adults, can arrive at the point of overturning an attitude prevalent in education. Adults need to fulfill their adult tasks without presenting themselves as the measure of everything and bring this to realization in the conviction that they are not the model of what the child must become.

The child is not a being that must be forged in the image of the adult; an image is imprinted in the child, but it is the image of God. The child is a person who lives a stage of life the characteristics of which we have perhaps forgotten.

The just attitude of the adult toward the child is, as Maria Montessori said, the attitude of a scientist, who observes the phenomenon of life and places himself or herself in the service of it with patience and humility—virtues, according to that great Italian educator, that are essential in every educator. The educator who is able to place himself or herself in such an attitude will find "something more than *interest in the phenomenon . . . will deduce from them the revelation of oneself, and one's emotions will vibrate at the contact with other souls like oneself*."[6]

Nevè Shalom/Wāhat al-Salām is a place unique in all the world, where peace, because of the care given to children, is being realized on solid foundations. When observing children in the nursery and school at Nevè Shalom/Wāhat al-Salām, we, the adults, can be guided to the true knowledge of the human person, discovering in ourselves treasures that are capable of building peace.

Nevè Shalom/Wāhat al-Salām is a vital place not only for Israel, but also for the whole world. Here we have wished to be interpreters of the world's gratitude to Father Bruno Hussar and all the coworkers in the village for the horizons of hope that they are opening for us all.

It seems to us that what we are seeing in Nevè Shalom/Wāhat al-Salām is the mysterious force of "the mustard seed" that the Gospel of Matthew speaks about (Matthew 13:31–32).

Endnotes

1. *Lettera dalla Collina* 12 (June 1995). Translator's note: This is the title of the publication put out by Nevè Shalom/Wāhat al-Salām, the community founded by Father Bruno Hussar and a group of laypersons.

2. Translator's note: Father Bruno Hussar (1911–1996) was an Egyptian-born Dominican priest of Jewish origin. He was able to realize his "dream" to provide a place in Israel where Jews, Christians, and Muslims might live in peace, with mutual respect for each other's faiths. Central to this community is the bilingual (Hebrew and Arabic) school for peace for children. Nominated for the Nobel Peace Prize, Father Hussar wrote about this "dream" in his book, *When the Cloud Lifted* (Ignatius Press, 1989).

3. Translator's note: For Psalm 65:2, many biblical translations use the word "answers" prayer (e.g., *New Revised Standard Version*, *Jerusalem Bible*); however, I have kept to the word Sofia uses: "hears," which is found in other translations (e.g., the *New American Bible*).

4. Dietrich Bonhoeffer, *Resistenza e Resa*, "Letter to Eberhard Bethge, 29 May 1944," Paoline Editoriale Libri 1988, 383. (See Dietrich Bonhoeffer, *Letters and Papers*

From Prison, The Enlarged Edition, ed. Eberhard Bethge (New York: Touchstone Book, 1997, 311–12.))

5. Maria Montessori, *Educazione e Pace*, Milan: Garzanti Libri Spa, 1970, 41. (See Part II: Educate for Peace, Sixth International Congress, "Address Opening the Conference" in *Education and Peace*, The Clio Montessori Series (Volume 10). Translated by Helen R. Lane, Oxford, England: Clio Press, 1992, 39.)

6. Maria Montessori, *L'Autoeducazione* (Garzanti, 1970), 120. This work appears under two titles in English: *Spontaneous Activity in Education* and *The Advanced Montessori Method: Volume One.* See "The Preparation of the Teacher," *The Advanced Montessori Method: Volume One*, trans. Florence Simmonds and Lily Hutchinson. (India: Kalakshetra Publications, 1965) 112.

Chapter Four

An Adventure: The Catechesis of the Good Shepherd

Translator's Note:
This essay was written in December 2001, for Muenster University. Sofia later wrote on the theme of "adventure" for those involved in the Good Shepherd Catechesis (see *Journal of the Catechesis of the Good Shepherd* 19 (2004)). In this essay we have a more substantial treatment, and it is, as Sofia writes in the final footnote of this chapter, "a brief synthesis" of her two volumes titled *The Religious Potential of the Child*, the first volume dedicated to the experience of catechesis with children under six and the second to children between the ages of six and 12.

In addition to the clarity and essentiality of her presentation, a striking aspect of this essay is that Sofia is writing it from the vantage point of 50 years on the "path," to which the *children* led them and guided their every step. That is at the heart of the "adventure."

This synthesis also serves as a comprehensive overview of the birth and growth of the Catechesis of the Good Shepherd. Additionally, Sofia makes explicit her debt to Dr. Maria Montessori (1870–1952), "that great educator," and specifically the ways in which the Catechesis has built on and developed some of Montessori's core educational principles.

A word about the endnotes in this chapter: Sofia has references to many works, which are retained as she wrote them in Italian. I have researched some of the English sources Sofia refers to, especially if she quotes an author more than once (Dietrich Bonhoeffer, for instance). When it might be unclear to an English audience as to which of Montessori's books Sofia is referring, I have given their English titles, and at times, more specific references. I have also added some notes, both to avoid inserting anything into

Sofia's text, as well to clarify a point or reference that cannot be assumed the reader will know; I have tried to keep these to a minimum.

Part I

Why speak of the Catechesis of the Good Shepherd as an "adventure"? There are two reasons. The first is because we are dealing with an experience, which, when we initiated it, we thought we were dedicating ourselves to a brief work, a parenthesis among other occupations. Instead, it became an impassioned undertaking of our whole lives, together with many other persons. We are speaking, therefore, of something that was not planned in advance; instead, it unfolded day by day, without our knowing where it would take us.

We say this at the start of this chapter in order to clarify immediately that it was not the adults, but rather the children (to be exact, children from two to three years of age)—who were, and are, the propelling force of this initiative. This is the first reason we can speak of this as an "adventure."

From the beginning of this initiative, the catechists found themselves in the presence of groups of children, and this experience stirred questions in us: Who are children in their relationship with God? How is a relationship like this configured? We observed the children and asked ourselves: Who are you?

From the very start, the catechists had the impression that they were coming close to the threshold of a most mysterious world: the relationship of God with his littlest creatures. This is the second, and principal reason, we can speak of an adventure: It was precisely a venturing into a world where everything was to be discovered. This is what David Hay means when he writes, "It may be the case that adults who attempt to comprehend the spirituality of children . . . may require some of the same skills as those employed by ethnographers investigating a culture remote from their own."[1]

Joy

This adventure had its beginning in Rome in 1954. We note this date because it is connected to the present moment by a "golden thread." That "golden thread" has always animated the Catechesis of the Good Shepherd, constitutes its spirit, and holds together all its history. It is what we will try to clarify in these pages.

There is a fundamental passage in the Gospel about the child's relationship with God: "for it is to such as these that the kingdom of God belongs. Truly I tell you, whoever does not receive the kingdom of God as a little child will never enter it" (Luke 18:16; Matthew 19:13; Mark 10:13). A great deal of ink has been poured exploring this text, including the works of illustrious scholars.[2] These studies usually highlight two aspects of the child's spirit: innocence and the disposition to believe.

We believe that we can add a third aspect to this list: the *joy* with which children live their relationship with God. We saw the first gleam of this reality right at the start in 1954, in the tears welling up in the eyes of a young boy as we came to the end of our first two-hour catechesis encounter; he was content and wanted to continue, or at least "to come every day."

That golden thread that interconnects the entire of the Catechesis of the Good Shepherd, that propelling force, as we said, which has carried forward almost a half-century of catechesis, is the *joy* of the child.

The joy of which we are speaking is a particular joy, a joy very different than the kind the child manifests in other positive experiences. We are speaking of an intense and recollected joy, which seems to touch the deepest chord in the child's spirit; the child appears to want to continue listening to its lingering vibrations. We are speaking of a joy in which the child manifests a total involvement, with the whole of his or her person, in an experience much like the joy of a one who has found one's own life-giving element. The child manifests a complete sense of satisfaction; the child is held in an enchanted silence, as though safeguarding an inner fermentation that is occurring within.

What is clear in these cases is the children's desire to prolong the experience, even if the exterior conditions change, without allowing

Gianna and Sofia in front of the cabinet dedicated to documentation, which also contains the collection of children's drawings. Photos by Patricia Coulter.

themselves to be distracted by them. What can be noticed is these cases are somewhat untypical affective manifestations, which show an overflowing of feelings. These manifestations are prolonged, even after the children leave the catechesis meetings. They are also expressed in the children's desire to be especially kind and gentle toward others, as they seek to interiorize this desire and try to live it out.

Manifestations like these resemble the phenomena which Montessori describes as moments when "the child begins to be completely transformed, to become more calm, almost more intelligent, more expansive; the child shows extraordinary interior qualities, which recall the phenomena of the highest level of conscience, like those found in conversion."[3]

Montessori calls these moments "polarization of attention." They are phenomena that unify the whole person in a sensation of total satisfaction, and they are produced when the child has found the food that responds to the deepest interior needs. We will return to this point later.

The Way

Young children seem to want to point out to us that *their* way of going to God is different, for example, from what is indicated in Thomas à Kempis's *Imitation of Christ*,[4] which originated in the medieval period and has been used to educate many generations up to recent times. It speaks about the "royal Way of the holy Cross" as the privileged path for going to God, whereas the child seems to wish to point out to us the "royal Way of holy Joy."

The path the child points out to us more closely resembles the one ardently desired by the Lutheran pastor Dietrich Bonhoeffer. He had observed how often religious people turn to God only when they hit up against their own limits, "or when human resources fail—in fact it is always the *deus ex machina* that they bring on to the scene, either for the apparent solution of insoluble problems, or as strength in human failure—always, that is to say, exploiting human weakness or human boundaries." Whereas what Bonhoeffer wishes is "to speak of God, not on the boundaries but at the center, not in weakness but in strength; and therefore not in death and guilt but in man's life and goodness."[5]

For the child, God is not a "stop-gap God," as Bonhoeffer phrases it, but someone to whom one goes in the fullness of one's whole person. Recent studies from the "The Religious Experience Research Unit" at Manchester College, Oxford, document the presence of joy in the religious experience of many people.[6] The research was conducted in great part through the correspondence of adults who recounted events they experienced at an early age. One person recalls "singing happily for hours" after religious services. Another affirms that participating in church services as a child "became a joy, a privilege, a delight." A correspondent from Vienna writes:

> Quite late in life I came to realize that my most significant religious experience had come when as a small child I was walking along my usual road in a built-up area in my hometown and, looking up, saw with inexpressible joy and thankfulness that the sky was blue . . . . It is joy in fact that is the basis of all life.[7]

This is also the basis upon which we have seen that the religious experience of the child is realized.

Prayer

The confirmation of what we said about the children's joy is found in the child's prayer, which is never the prayer of petition, at least when the adult has not led the child to this form of prayer. The genuine prayer of the child, especially the young child, has no magical aspect to it, that is, the child does not ask for the resolution of problems.

Instead, the child's prayer consists in enjoying the encounter with Someone whom the child can "tell about the good things of the day" (seven-year-old girl, Italy). The child's prayer is not an expression that arises from the awareness of a need, of something that is lacking, or from a situation of suffering; instead, it takes the form of pure praise and thanksgiving. Consider the example of the three-year-old girl (Italy) who, sitting down to the dinner table, said: "Goodness, light. Amen." Or the prayer of a five-year-old boy who expressed himself this way: "I say to him: Alleluia to the mighty God." One child (Italy) in a group of children between the

Sofia with child in the atrium in the 1970s. Photographer unknown.

ages of four and six voiced this: "Jesus, you are great, you are good, you are beautiful; you are for me a jewel."

One eight-year-old girl (with Down's syndrome) began the prayer of a group of four-to-six-year-old children with these words: "Thank you for the light." The other children followed, each expressing their gratitude, linked to a variety of reasons; then the girl who began the prayer time ended it by saying: "My body is happy." A two-and-a-half-year-old girl (USA) was already in bed, and said to herself: "Jesus loves me, Jesus loves me, Holy Spirit, God, Jesus loves me, Holy Spirit, God. Alleluia."

Another five-year-old child (USA) expressed gratitude to God in this way: "Thank you, God, for me; thank you, God, for you; thank you for the light." An older child, seven years of age (USA), prayed, "God is Savior, God of heaven, God of light, God of the world, God of the earth, God of love, holy God, God who sees us."

And if we want to look for a prayer of petition, here is one from a young boy belonging to the three to six age group (USA): "Let me do, Lord, something like a bath in your light."

These expressions all indicate serene enjoyment, which comes from a richness, from a "fullness" that is meant to be enjoyed, and certainly not from an "emptiness" that asks to be filled up.

The child reaches these levels, which we have tried to highlight, independently from the adult. One mother wished to make her three-year-old child pray, and the child (Mexico) responded: "I pray alone and in silence."

It is the independence seen in a child of five (Italy) who asked his mother, a self-professed atheist: "Who do you love more, me or God?" When he received the answer, "You of course," he observed, "I think that is your big mistake."

This is the child whom we have seen. This is the child of whom it has been said that there is no "being more metaphysical."[8] This is the child who has guided us in our work, the child who seems to find in the relationship with God that "fullness of being" which Rudolf Bultmann speaks of, and that "pleasing sense of joy and of new dignity," as Montessori expressed it.[9]

Part II
Growth

For the first decade or so, our work took place in a generally uniform social environment; therefore, it might be thought that the children's responses were determined in some way by the environment in which they lived. This social uniformity, however, was accompanied by a remarkable religious diversity, in the sense that we were working with children who belonged to more or less practicing Catholic families, as well as to freethinking families or to families of self-professed atheist parents.

The aspect of social uniformity ended when the Good Shepherd Catechesis spread to children who were from lower middle and working class families, as well as to gypsies. In spite of this diversity, the response continued to be the same.

In 1975 the Catechesis spread into even more diverse environments when the first North American courses were given in Minneapolis, Minnesota, and then in Mexico the following year. This enabled us to come into contact with increasingly more diverse communities. The

Catechesis spread from culturally refined families to children from the impoverished outskirts of major cities, and also to indigenous people (for example, of the Sierra di Puebla) who belonged to groups that were still illiterate or in the process of becoming literate.

In addition, this was not limited to Catholic environments; rather, the Catechesis began to spread quickly to various sister churches, first to the Episcopal, then to the Lutheran, and to other denominations as well. Now we are present in 20 countries: in Europe, from North, Central, and South America to Australia.

The Child

In all of these diverse environments the child's response has always been the same and refers us back to what was said above: it is a response composed of complete satisfaction, meditative silence, and deep joy. The golden thread was ever-lengthening, uniting together thousands of children from very diverse milieux and situations, but the response to the religious experience never changed.

Faced with such an impressive uniformity of response, we began to think that what was taking shape before our eyes might be *the child*—the human being in the first stages of life—in his or her relationship with God in all its genuineness, beyond social or educational conditioning. In addition, it needs to be noted that we are speaking about children who live in a variety of different conditions: of personal or familial suffering, in serene environments and in environments of conflict, in institutions and in hospitals.

In other words, at the end of this quick review of the spread of the Good Shepherd Catechesis, we would like to observe that we find ourselves facing a phenomenon, in which there are two seemingly contradictory elements:

1) an ever-growing number of children (two to 12 years of age) who live in the most diverse environments and situations, and

2) at the same time, there is the evidence that all these children respond to the religious factor, and always respond to it in the same way.

That is to say, there is a counter-positioning between the diversification in the milieux and situations in which the children live and the constant uniformity in their response to the religious reality.

An observable fact like this leads us to affirm that the circumstances—positive or negative—in which the children might be living do not reach the level of, or touch, their relationship with God, a relationship which appears to be situated, within the child's person, at a level that is different from the child's daily experiences.

Every experience of daily life arises from one or more external causes, which are interiorized and then generate different reactions and influence the person to a more or less profound degree. The child's experience of the relationship with God is different from these; it does not appear to derive from external factors which, by their very nature, are diverse and thus would produce different results from person to person.

The child's relationship with God seems prior to and independent of any external factors whatsoever; it is something that is stronger than such experiences and unassailable by them; the religious reality seems to be located at a deeper level than educational interventions of whatever type. It is something that cannot be taught. It seems to be birthed from virgin ground; it manifests itself as something primordial, something that springs directly from one unique source.

This uniqueness of source would explain the uniformity of response on the part of children, which we have verified. We wish to speak of a *vital need,* to which the person's whole being is directed and, when it encounters the food that corresponds to this vital need, the person's whole being finds satisfaction. By that we mean to say something that resembles David Hay's observation: "My scientific conviction [is] that spirituality, in all its scope, inclusive of religious consciousness, is totally natural . . . [and] is of fundamental importance for human survival."[10]

All this prompts us to attempt a first response to the question we asked ourselves at the start: Who is the child? Who are you?

Children appear to have found their vital, life-giving environment in the religious reality, which seems to indicate to us that there is a *connaturality* at the origin of their relationship with God. Children manifest such ease in the religious relationship, live it with such spontaneity and profundity at the same time, and with such independence from the adult, that we said to ourselves: *like attracts like.*

This is the reason, in our estimation, for that total satisfaction that the child manifests in the religious reality. This is the reason for that constant and uniform response in the religious experience that we have seen on the part of children.

A response like this does not depend on particular didactic programs or on special pedagogical advances. These can surely be helpful, but they would serve nothing were the child not what it is: a creature who is privileged in the relationship with God. It is not insignificant that Jesus singled out the young child as the particular citizen in the Kingdom and proposed the child as the model of the Kingdom.

We might say that among the four types of soil upon which the sower scattered seed (Matthew 13:1ff.), the child is the one that produces a hundredfold. This is the mystery of the child; this is the great joy of the adult: to help—with wonder, growing joy, and gratitude—the miracle of this extraordinary vegetation, and to realize that we are "merely servants" (Luke 17:10) to whom has been granted the gift of being its witnesses.

Part III
The Adult

The catechist's joy is not disconnected from "fear and trembling" in the face of the mystery of God's relationship with the child; the more one is aware of the greatness of this reality, the more one feels inadequate to the task of catechist.

This connaturality between God and the child is a hidden treasure in the "most secret core" of the soul, that "sanctuary" within the human person where one "is alone with God whose voice echoes in [one's] depths."[11] No one is given the right to try to enter this sanctuary. The help we may give to the child's potentialities can be and should be an indirect aid only. Montessori distinguishes between what she calls "a center and a periphery":

> The center belongs to the individual . . . . Whereas the periphery, which puts the individual in contact with the external world through the senses

and to which the individual responds with one's movement, yes, this is accessible to us. We can reach the periphery; we see the child reacting and expressing himself or herself through his or her activities. We can see this. Therefore we base ourselves on this.[12]

The Atrium

The first indirect aid we can give is to create an environment that helps the child work independently of the adult as far as possible, as a way for the child to manifest who he or she truly is.

Religious life is an attitude that permeates the whole of one's personality and the whole of one's life, but it also needs a place in which it can be lived with greater intentionality. From most ancient times humankind has felt the necessity of preparing places of worship, and in our own day our cities are rich in churches from various different epochs.

Churches are special environments for the religious life of children as well. But, besides the church, children—who have shown that they live the relationship with God in a way that is their own—need a place in which to prepare, according to their own rhythm and capacities, to live the life of the Church together with adults. Children need a place committed to this purpose: this place is what Montessori called "atrium." Atrium refers to the intermediate space in the ancient basilicas, which served as an antechamber, in the material and metaphorical sense, to the place of worship.[13] Montessori wanted an intermediate space of this nature—between classroom and church—to be found in schools as well.

We realize that it is very difficult to explain what an atrium is to someone who has never seen one. The atrium is beautiful when it is inhabited by children—silent, concentrated, working happily, unceasingly, like worker bees. The children create such an intense atmosphere that the atrium then speaks all on its own.

The atrium is a place where a community of children lives a religious experience together with some adults (the catechists) that prepares them to participate in the larger family community, ecclesial and social. In the atrium, the children are initiated into the realities of the Christian life, but also, and above all, they begin to live this life in meditation and prayer.

Gianna, Sofia, and Luigi Capogrossi, President of the Maria Montessori Association for the Religious Formation of the Child, Rome. Photographer unknown.

The atrium is different from a classroom in a school. In the atrium, there is no teacher's desk or chair, because there is only one Teacher, to whose voice the adult and children together are listening.

The catechist is not a professor of religion. The atrium is not a place of *religious instruction,* but of *religious life.* It resembles a classroom in that it is a place of work and study; in the atrium, however, work and study become colloquy with God, and therefore it is already a place of worship in some sense. In the atrium, children can live according to their own rhythm, something not possible in church, when the whole community is gathered.

The atrium is certainly a place of learning, but it is learning that has a predominantly celebratory character, in which learning is deschooled, in the sense that there is no need for those instruments that are generally used in school, such as marks, testing, exams, assigned tasks, or homework. All customary means of academic control are renounced in the atrium, precisely in respect for that one Teacher of whom we spoke, who "dwells within the intimate" part of us, in Saint Augustine's words, and teaches us in that intimate place, which precludes any direct intervention on the adult's part.[14]

The Material

In order for catechesis to be catechesis and not a religion lesson, it is necessary that catechesis be deschooled. Rather than resembling a class, the atrium should be more like a spiritual retreat center, where many things can be found to help concentration and prayer, and on an individual level.

In a retreat center, for example, there are books that can be of special help to the adult in moments of personal reflection. The atrium also has books for children who are already able to read, but there is what we call the "material" as well. The material, which we will now try to describe, constitutes the second indirect aid we can provide to help children in their mysterious relationship with God.

Let us say at the outset that we are not speaking about a didactic material, according to the usual usage of that word; namely, material that is designed by adults to make our own presentation of a theme more effective. The material of the atrium is Montessorian in character, and thus it is understood as an aid in continuing the child's meditation [usually on a presentation on a Scripture passage or aspect of the liturgy]. This meditation was begun together with the adult, but the atrium allows the child's listening to the interior Teacher to be prolonged, in full independence of the adult.

In the very simple material the children find all the elements of the theme (that has been presented earlier) in tactile form, made in wood or paper, which are easily manipulated, as well as what is available in written form for the older children. Learning does not happen only with the mind, but also with the touch.

For example, the material for the Good Shepherd parable is made up of a wooden base, on top of which is an enclosure, representing a sheepfold, and two-dimensional wooden figures, one of a shepherd and ten sheep. The material must contain all the elements of the theme presented, without additions which the catechist might consider as embellishments; the material must be strictly objective, simple, and essential—sober to the point that it could seem poor. Anyone would be capable of making it with their own hands.

"Embellishments" to the material do not tend to concentrate the child's attention or bring into clear relief the content of the texts presented, and could be obstacles to direct contact with the texts.

The value of the material consists in the richness of the contents, not in the exterior form, and even less in an assumed inventiveness on the part of the catechist. A material about which a catechist could say, "What a great find I've made!" is a misdirected material. What strikes one in the material is the incommensurability between such simple means which nonetheless manage to express such great realities.

This leads us to reflect on how very great the simplest things are. But it is exactly in the contrast between simplicity and greatness that we adults lose our way. When it seems necessary to us to complicate simple things— as though they were lacking something—we obfuscate their greatness.

After the adult's presentation of the theme, the material is at the disposition of the children, who choose freely what they wish to work with and the length of time they wish to do so.

The material is also helpful because it allows the adult to know the children—their interests, their rhythm of working—when they are free to act on their own, rather than according to the adult's expectations of them. For example, we will see that children under six years of age will return again and again to the same material, without becoming tired. On the other hand, the older children will search for materials which help them to return to a certain theme but view it from different angles.

Therefore, the material helps the catechist to be more aware that one is "merely servant," as we said, in the sense that one's task is limited to the first moment of learning, namely, to indicate a particular theme. But that is not when the learning happens. As Saint Augustine reminds us: "I can never teach" (*Quia ego numquam possum docere*). According to Saint Augustine, it is only "when they who are called pupils, consider in the inner court of the mind what has been said . . . only then do they learn (*tunc ergo discunt*)."[15]

Boethius said, "Through teaching, the mind is only stimulated to know; but the one who stimulates the other to know is not capable of making the other know, just as the person who stimulates the eye to see is incapable of making the eye see; thus, one person is incapable of making another know."[16]

The catechist is a poor person who has the greatest wealth in his or her hands, a richness that does not belong to oneself. With respect to this, the document *On Catechesis in Our Time* cites Jesus' words (John 7:16): "Every catechist should be able to apply to oneself the mysterious words of Jesus: 'My teaching is not mine, but his who sent me.'"[17]

The material, as we said, repositions the catechist in the sense that it clarifies the nature of the catechist's place and task; in the second moment of learning, the catechist must move aside, must be as discreet as possible, so that the child's contact can be established with the true Teacher.[18] It is to this direct contact that both the environment and material are oriented. Then the adult's "fear and trembling" gives way to a profound respect for the mysterious colloquy between God and the child, and also to a wondrous joy in beholding what is sometimes given to one to see.

Montessori said that every child is addressing a silent request to the adult: "Help me to do it by myself." Certainly, the child needs the adult and does ask for help. The help we give, however, must be such that we do not substitute ourselves for the child, thus denigrating the child, but rather we encourage the child to express these potentialities in all their richness.

For catechists, that child for whom God is searching "as like seeks like," that "metaphysical" child, is asking us without words: "Help me to come close to God by myself."

Part IV
Method

Now we will address the themes we present to children, indicating the criteria and methodology we use in the presentations. Obviously, it is not possible to present all the themes in this short space, and so we will point out one theme that we propose to children under the age of six, and one for children between six and 12 years of age.

In reference to methodology, what we most wish to underscore is that a method is not an instrument without a soul, which can be used indifferently with regard to any content whatsoever. If the content does not find the method congenial to it, there is a risk that the method will deform it.

In observing children, we soon realized that the language of signs was the one to be adopted—that language which is more visual than auditory, in which there are few words—so as to allow the gestures and concrete objects to speak. Children are extremely capable of perceiving—we could say of contemplating—the Mystery behind this language. The language of signs is the language that the liturgy has always spoken, and which has become less comprehensible in our time, due to the lack of initiation into their meaning.

The Bible has also always spoken through signs. The Bible recounts the histories of the people of God through events. These events are to be considered in their evident meaning, and also sounded to their depths, so as to perceive the presence and action of God within them and within the whole of history.

The Bible and the liturgy thus speak the same language. The common element is that both are allusive languages. That is, neither the Bible nor liturgy exhausts the richness of the content they contain; rather, they urge us forward on a path whose end we do not see, and that is why it is so attractive to us. We are dealing with a language which is understood only very gradually and which opens incommensurable horizons before us.

In contrast to *definitions,* which claim to define, and thereby limit their content, biblical-liturgical language knows that its contents are greater than the container, because in bringing us close to the Mystery it cannot speak other than by means of allusions. Therefore, we were not bound to go and research complicated methods, but only to use that method which has always been present in the tradition of the Church.

For example, in presenting Baptism to children, we had to do nothing other than to lift into focus the signs of the baptismal liturgy (water, Word, light, white garment, and so on) and to introduce these signs in a certain gradual process. The signs spoke a language with such clarity that, through them, the theology of the sacrament emerged in all its richness. We allowed the signs to speak: they drew forth from the children those qualities of delight and wonder that made their eyes light up, as though they were looking beyond the materiality of the objects and seeing through to the Mystery they were indicating.

Themes

With the passage of time we came to realize that some themes were perceived with particular intensity and joy by children in the three to six age group, others in the six to eight age group, and still others in the nine to 12 age group. These themes were the ones for which the children had an insatiable hunger. They returned constantly to the materials for these and responded to them with such seriousness and depth, as we tried to describe above. This was how a list of themes began to take shape, the themes that seemed to respond most fully to the vital needs of children at the various age levels.

We did exactly as a mother would do in deciding what food is good for her child. A mother tries out a certain kind of food and then watches her child's reaction; if the child is well, grows, and receives what is given with pleasure, then that is the right food for that child.

For us, the means of measuring the "food" to give children is the joy with which they receive it. Montessori established an interesting relation between growth and joy. She said, "Joy is the indicator of interior growth, as weight gain is the indicator of the growth of the body."[19]

Therefore, in forming a list of the themes, nothing was preprogrammed, nothing in the nature of devising a list (according to our way of thinking) and then passing it on to the children.

The journey was traveled in the opposite direction. The emerging themes were selected only after being sifted through a sieve: that is to say, after researching the reason for their reception by the children in terms of the psychology of the various developmental stages, and after examining the themes that were taking shape in the light of the biblical sources and the liturgical and patristic traditions. Thus the journey took this direction: traveling from the "fieldwork" with children to our study at the desk and work tables.

The Christian Message

At a certain moment, we realized that with a sure hand the children had guided us to the essential points of the Christian message, those same points which have remained present in the tradition of the Church from the first centuries.

Thus our work consisted in stripping away many secondary elements we were giving to the children (to which the children remained indifferent and the materials languished on the shelves), to concentrate on the essential, that "essential" Franz Marc spoke of this way: "The spiritual life is to distinguish the essential from what is not."[20]

This search for the essential led us to change paths more than once and to eliminate superfluous materials. And so we found ourselves with a framework, to which we adults contributed our doctrinal and methodological knowledge, but in a way that had been developed and directed by the children.

We understood the logic of this framework only *post eventum*, and we found ourselves before it as a gift that God had given us through the child. At this point that "fear and trembling" about which we spoke gave way to the joy of gratitude.

Sources

We recognized, with wonder, that the themes which the children receive with such naturalness, depth, and joy are the greatest ones. In these themes are contained all that is essential in the Christian message in its greatest expressions, so great that we established a guideline: "give the greatest to the littlest."

We did this with only one exception: the theme of history as presented in its globality (about which we will say more later). Children under the age of six do not have the capability of orienting themselves to the dimension of time, and thus they cannot grasp the grandeur of history, that aspect in which the older children (beginning around the age of six or seven) take such delight.

Essentiality has been a hard school for us adults—who easily fall into secondary elements—and the road has been long, but worth following. Essentiality led us to objectivity, that is, to the elimination of personal attitudes in our work with children, such as preferences for certain devotions or personal embellishments, which may be important for us personally but which risk usurping the place of the essentiality of the message. In a certain sense, we need to hide ourselves behind the message, so as not to obfuscate its force, and to place only the message in the light. It is in this way alone that we will be able to see the force and the power of the Word of God.

What needs to be given and offered in measured doses to the children are the sources, i.e., the Bible and the liturgy. These sources are what give rise to the personal reflections in the fecund exchange between child and adult. It is in this exchange that we become aware of the level of profundity that the "metaphysical" child reaches, even in response to texts that seemed too arduous for children.

Bible

Among all the themes proposed to the youngest children (under six years of age), what immediately stood out was the parable of the Good Shepherd (John 10:1ff.). This parable is composed of three parts. The first and the third parts present Jesus as the shepherd, while the second part introduces the image of the "gate of the sheepfold" (verses 7–10). We concentrate on the first and third parts with young children.

Generally, the part that is most cited is usually the third part, which emphasizes the shepherd's giving of his life for his sheep and the shepherd who said, "I have the power to lay it down, and I have the power to take it up again" (John 10:18). Children almost never refer to this element, with a few rare exceptions.

Instead, their activity and artwork is flooded with the image of the shepherd in the act of calling his sheep by name. In their drawings or their writings (when they are able to write or when they ask that an adult write for them), a name will appear above each lamb. Or there will be that balloon-shaped image issuing from the mouth of Jesus, filled with all the names of the "sheep" he is calling. There are also constant references to this first part of the parable in their verbal exchanges.

It is clear that what most strikes the young child in this text is the personal relationship that exists between the Shepherd and the sheep. It is a well-known fact that relationship is a vital need essential in the living of human life. From the collection of children's artwork (about a thousand drawings) in the Center of the Good Shepherd catechesis in Rome, it is evident that the feeling of relationship called forth from the parable is strong, and that from various drawings of children ages six and younger, who are from different countries and cultures, the relationship between Shepherd and sheep is linked to the relationship that unites the mother and child in the prenatal stage of life.

In a drawing by a two-and-a-half-year-old child (USA), the sheep is represented by a circle that is inscribed inside a larger circle, and the child explained that the larger one is the Good Shepherd and the smaller one is the sheep. It has been possible to interpret this drawing in the light of other drawings by children a little older (five- to six-year-olds, in Mexico, Italy), who, because they have greater graphic abilities, have represented the Shepherd as a mother with the child in the womb.

Children's artwork is a precious mine for knowing their psychological reactions and their capacities of theological intuition and—I do not hesitate to use this word—exegesis.

If we consider that "relationship" is the generic term which the biblical language expresses as "covenant" (in Hebrew, *berith;* in Greek, *diatheke*), we will recognize how children have taken hold of an element of utmost psychological importance and which is fundamental in biblical theology.[21] According to Salvatore Natoli, "Judaic religiousness [we must also add Christian] in its substantial dynamism would remain incomprehensible apart from the idea of the covenant."[22]

The God of the Bible is the "God in search of man."[23] This God searches to have a relationship with us, seeks to establish a covenant relationship with us, wants to attract us to himself by various means, which in the Book of Jeremiah is synthesized by the term "enticement" (Jeremiah 20). Thus, we are at the heart of the biblical message.[24]

We can say that every time we see children enjoying the Good Shepherd parable, whether it is hearing it read to them, working with the materials of the parable, or working on a drawing on this theme, we are witness to a wonderful sight: the birth and growth of the covenant between

God and the child. The child, without words, is expressing himself or herself as Jeremiah did: "O Lord, you have enticed me, and I was enticed" (20:7).

The fact that the Good Shepherd image does not correspond with any concrete person who might be in the children's lives, allows the children to be less encumbered and thus freer to receive the voice that is calling in the depths of their being.

"What is the Good Shepherd calling his sheep to?" a catechist asks of a group of the youngest children. The response they gave was: "To life."

In speaking of the covenant, one usually thinks immediately of God's initiative, which requests a response on the part of the human creature. This response is generally conceived on the level of what to do and not to do; that is, according to a reductionist conception of the moral element, which often limits it to the observance of a code of laws.

This element is certainly present in the moral life, but it is not the only one. There is a response that precedes it and constitutes in every stage of life the essential basis for the observance of any norm. It is precisely the response that we alluded to earlier with Jeremiah's term: enticement. It is to allow oneself to be enticed, to enjoy being sought after, to enjoy the relationship that is coming to birth, to know ourselves as "called to life" by a voice that we recognize (John 10:4). This is the response we have seen in the children.

Liturgy

The "covenant" is presented by means of the liturgy, as well as through the biblical sources. For instance, the initiation of the youngest children to the Eucharist occurs through a long, slow process comprised of different steps. It eventually leads to the point where the older children know the complete Eucharistic ritual as contained in the missal.

In this process we make use of the language of signs, by means of which, as we said, even the youngest children read the most profound theological contents with great facility, contents which we would have much difficulty presenting with words alone.

In presenting the Eucharist, "the sacrament of the new and everlasting covenant,"[25] we present certain gestures to children. The first is the epiclesis (invocation to the Father to send the Spirit), which precedes the account of the Last Supper. The gesture is the imposition of the priest's hands over the Eucharistic species, indicating that this is the gift that comes from above.

The other gesture occurs at the end of the Eucharistic prayer, when the priest's hands, which hold the consecrated Bread and Wine, are lifted up. This gesture lets us "see" the gesture of offering, in response to the gift received.

These complementary gestures show the two moments of the covenant in the living reality of the celebration.

Our method could be called a "spiral" method. That is to say, it is a method that resembles what happens when a stone is thrown into water: first, it reaches to the deepest point, and, then, its presence is signaled by the gradual formation of ever-widening concentric circles on the water's surface. In the Good Shepherd catechesis, the deepest level is reached with the youngest children. While always keeping that point in view, the horizons are then expanded with the older children.

With wonder, we come to recognize that, while this nucleus grows gradually larger over the years, its deepest level has already been reached by the youngest children.

By presenting the covenant through the biblical sources and the liturgical tradition, we attain that unity between Bible and liturgy which is underlined in the Second Vatican Council, particularly in the *Constitution on the Sacred Liturgy (Sacrosanctum Concilium)*.[26]

Time

Around the age of six or seven years of age, children are entering into a new phase of life. This is indicated by physical elements, for instance, as in the change in teeth. A phrase commonly used to name this stage, "the age of reason," is actually an inappropriate expression, in that it seems to presuppose that there is no reason in the child before this time. But at this time the capacities of knowing and learning are being integrated with other, newer capacities, such as the tendency toward abstract thought, a new interest in rules, and the ability to distinguish clearly what is good and not good, and so forth.

Less is said about another very important acquisition at this age: the ability to orient oneself in time. According to Jean Piaget, this capacity surfaces a little later,[27] whereas Montessori indicates its beginning around six or seven years of age. The ability to orient oneself in time is extremely important for communication.

In addition, it is indispensable for the exercise of our intellectual capacities, because "thinking cannot be dissociated from the thrust of time," that thrust which "is present in every phenomenon that can be perceived, from an atom of hydrogen to the most complex phenomena,"[28] and it becomes more evident as one gradually rises to more complex levels.

Time, therefore, is a cosmic dimension which the human creature shares with other elements of creation and which in some way renders the human person in solidarity with these created elements. Time is a human phenomenon and cosmic fundamental. Beyond this, "temporality offers us a transparency on the eternal."[29]

History

We are not speaking, of course, of proposing a theoretical discourse on time to children. Nor does the Bible give us a philosophy on time.[30] The Bible offers us "an intelligence of history"[31]; that is, a vast and profound penetration into history, a capacity to sound its events in their depth, and so to discover a level within them that goes beyond such events. The prophet, who is the exponent of Hebrew spirituality, is an interpreter of history.[32]

The Bible tells us two extremely significant things about time and history. Most importantly, it tells us that time is not empty, but that it is indwelt by a presence. This is the presence of the One Lord, who makes One history: connecting together all the various events into a unity, the Lord is guiding history with love toward a goal—the *telos* of Saint Paul (1 Corinthians 15:24) when even the ultimate enemy, death, will be conquered.

Thus time—as distinct from *kronos,* which devours everything—follows a linear movement. History is "cumulative" history, and it is history with a destination.

As with every kind of history, biblical history is composed of light and shadow. Yet, unlike other kinds of history, we are told how this biblical history will conclude. It will not continue on in an indefinite alternation between positive and negative; instead, the light will overcome the darkness.

Certainly the prophets did not ignore the contradictions, conflicts, and also the regressions of history. The Bible, however, tells us that the unfolding of events which, if only seen superficially could seem disconnected, is held together by a thread and is part of the plan of God "so that God may be all in all" (1 Corinthians 15:28). History teaches us a fundamental biblical virtue: hope.

We must keep in mind, however, an aspect that is sometimes not attended to in catechesis: namely, that before dealing with various individual histories, there is *the* history. Before coming to the single events, we need to give children the overarching sense of the globality of biblical history in all its richness: it originates at the beginning of time, at creation, and it moves toward its conclusion, toward what the Bible calls "the end of the age," eschatology.

It is this global aspect of time that is the perspective in which older children will come to read the individual events. It is only upon this foundation that children will take hold of the full meaning of these events.

The History of the Kingdom of God[33]

This global aspect is treated in three successive steps with children between the ages of six and eight. For lack of space here, we will only describe the first step, which is intended to highlight for the children the length and grandeur of the history narrated in the Bible, that it is a unique history, yet, in spite of its immense proportions, it is the history of each one of us.

This first presentation is accompanied by a timeline strip 50 meters long, which is intended for the personal work of the children. Each thread in the strip represents 1,000 years, more or less. The timeline indicates the beginning at creation. Then there is the appearance of *homo sapiens,* followed by a relatively short space of the strip to the point which marks the moment of redemption. The 2,000 years that separate us from that moment seem such a short span of time when seen in light of the history that preceded it.

After the point that marks the present day comes the white section of the timeline representing the history that is still yet to be realized. This is the "blank page" that each of us must write so that history will attain its fulfillment: the Parousia.

What impresses the children in this theme is the great contrast between the dimensions of history and the littleness of our presence in it. "How do you feel in front of this history?" an adult asks a group of children. Some of them said, "small," but one of them affirmed, "great." The grandeur of this reality makes our littleness more obvious but, at the same time, this littleness is exalted in the discovery that each of one us is in some way part of such a great reality.

This theme helps us to take the "measure" of God and of ourselves, so to speak. The greatness of the human person is strongly underlined in the Bible, and the mystery of time is an important perspective from which to see the place of the human person in its true light.

The flow of time and history engages each person who enters it, in his or her own greatness. To be part of such a great history confers dignity. When taking the human person into consideration, it is necessary never to lose sight of the two poles of reference, but rather to place our gaze simultaneously on the greatness and the littleness, on God and on the human creature.

It is from the disproportion between these two poles that wonder is born, an essential source for the spiritual life. Then we will recognize that what ought to separate these two poles instead unites them in a mysterious bond. We discover that the incommensurability between them gives us the measure of the love of God.

Humility and Hope

These considerations educate us in that virtue which has been called the "cardinal Christian virtue": humility. This virtue helps us to take our rightful place in reality. It is a difficult virtue because between its two poles—God and the human creature—the prevailing tendency is to look primarily at the second pole, the human and our limitations.

In doing so, we obscure what is foremost in this virtue. Humility is the virtue which "takes our eyes off our sinfulness . . . to turn them towards God's goodness and mercy." This is the virtue which "directs the heart to what is above," and which is expressed "in wonder and exultation," according to Saint Augustine.[34]

It is that virtue which Saint John of the Cross synthesized in the words:

> Your eyes in mine aglow
> printed their living image in my own.
> *Spiritual Canticle,* 23[35]

In the response of the older children to the presentation of this theme, we note those same manifestations which can be observed in the youngest children's response to the Good Shepherd parable: concentration, happy and passionate work without becoming tired, an attentive silence, and the desire to return to the theme for longer periods of time. These are manifestations that indicate when a deep spring has been touched, and when the exterior stimuli correspond to interior needs.

It can also be observed how older children have the capacity to connect the presentations on history with other themes they already know. Fabrizio (eight years of age, Rome), made a timeline four meters long, on which he inserted various elements: geophysical, biological, the primitive history of humanity. Then he illustrated the moment of the Parousia with the figure of the Good Shepherd along with numerous sheep.

Children often connect these presentations on history with the parables, for example, to the mustard seed, or to the precious pearl that we all will possess at the Parousia, and so forth.

The global framework of history constantly remains the indispensable foundation for knowing about its individual events, for being able to grasp the connection that links them all together, and the dynamism that carries history toward its eschatological fulfillment. In other words, the grandeur of this framework is the necessary instrument so that we can gradually enter into the thought of God.

Moral Education

We cannot explicitly address the theme of moral education, even though the parenetic element[36] clearly constitutes an important part of the Catechesis of the Good Shepherd. We wish, however, to clarify that, even though we have limited our discussion here to the kerygma—the Christian message—we have been speaking about moral formation at the same time; in fact, the kerygma is the most solid base upon which to situate it. For example, in speaking about the Good Shepherd parable, we have emphasized how children read it as a parable of covenant, and, as we all know, relationship is the essential foundation of the moral life.

A second example: In speaking about the globality of history, we have seen how it orients us toward two foundational attitudes [of the moral life]: hope and humility. And we could multiply the examples.

The richness of the Judeo-Christian kerygma is such that it speaks on its own, even before any kind of parenesis whatsoever. We must not obfuscate the richness of the kerygma with untimely parenetic interventions. This would risk impeding the enjoyment of the message that the Bible gives us, and it would confuse the very face of God.

The foundation of the moral life is "enticement." The foundation of the moral life is that joy which, from its first beginnings, has been the propelling force of the "adventure" of the Catechesis of the Good Shepherd.[37]

Endnotes

1. David Hay and Rebecca Nye, *The Spirit of the Child* (London: Jessica Kingsley Publishers, 2006), p. 83. See also Norbert Mette, "Learning to Live and Believe with Children," *Concilium* 2 (1996), pp. 99–110.

2. I limit myself to Simon Légasse, *Jésus et L'Enfant: "Enfants," "Petits" et "Simples" dans la Tradition Synoptique* (Paris: Gabalda, 1970).

3. Maria Montessori, *L'Autoeducazione*: Nelle Scuole Elementari (Milan: Garzanti, 1970), p. 61, 83. (Translator's note: This book appears under two titles in English: *Spontaneous Activity in Education* and *The Advanced Montessori Method: Volume One*. See Chapter III, "My Contribution to Experimental Science" in *The Advanced Montessori Method: Volume One* (Madras, India: Kalakshetra Publications, 1965)).

4. Thomas à Kempis, *Imitation of Christ,* II; XII.

5. Italo Mancini, *Bonhoeffer* (Florence, Italy: Vallecchi, 1969), p. 374 ff. (Translator's note: See Letter to Eberhard Bethge, 30 April 1944, in *Dietrich Bonhoeffer: Letters and Papers from Prison,* ed. Eberhard Bethge (New York: Touchstone, 1997), pp. 281–2).

6. Edward Robinson, *The Original Vision: A Study of the Religious Experience of Childhood* (New York: Seabury Press, 1983), p. 97; 136.

7. Viktor Frankl makes what seems to be an interesting observation in relation to particular cases in which patients that "were known to be manifestly irreligious" recount "flagrantly religious dreams." He notes, "What is most striking in such dreams is an ecstatic experience of bliss that was unknown to the patient in his waking life. It is simply impossible to insist that behind such an experience there must be a sexual meaning . . . " *Dio nell' inconsio* (Brescia: Morcelliana, 1990), p. 76. (Translator's note: This essay was published in English as "The Unconscious God" in 1975. More recently it has been published as *Man's Search for Ultimate Meaning* (New York: Basic Books, 2000), p. 69–70).

8. Andre Frossard in *Le Figaro,* August 10, 1970: "There are no children other than those that are truly metaphysical."

9. Maria Montessori, *I Bambini Viventi Nella Chiesa* (Milan: Garzanti, 1970), p. 15. (Maria Montessori, *The Child in the Church,* ed. E. M. Standing (Saint Paul, MN: Catechetical Guild, 1965), p. 24).

10. David Hay and Rebekah Nye, *The Spirit of the Child,* p. 146; 153.

11. *The Church in the Modern World (Gaudium et Spes),* Part One, No. 16 in *Vatican Council II: The Conciliar and Post Conciliar Documents,* ed. Austin Flannery, OP (New York: Costello Publishing Company, 1975), p. 917.

12. Maria Montessori, *I Bambini che Belle Persone!* Centro Nascita Montessori (Como: Red, 1995), IX.

13. Maria Montessori, *I Bambini Viventi Nella Chiesa,* p. 9–19. (Translator's note: See "The Atrium," *The Child in the Church,* ed. E. M. Standing (Saint Paul, MN: Catechetical Guild, St. Paul, 1965), p. 32–44).

14. Saint Augustine, *De Magistro,* XIV [*On the Teacher,* Ch. 14]. (Translator's note: See *The Philosophy of Teaching: A Study in the Symbolism of Language, A Translation of St. Augustine's "De Magistro,"* trans. Fr. Francis E. Tourscher (Villanova, PA: Villanova College, 1924)).

15. *Ibid.* (Translator's note: "But all these branches of learning, which teachers profess to teach . . . when they have explained them by means of words; then they who are called pupils, consider in the inner court of the mind whether what has been said is true, that is, in the measure of their own mental power they see the truth that is within. Then, therefore, they learn.")

16. Boethius, *De Consolatione Philosophiae (The Consolation of Philosophy), Book V, 5,* cited by St. Thomas, *De Veritate,* Q. XI, no. 12 *passim.*

17. *On Catechesis in Our Time (Catechesi Tradendae),* No. 6. Rome, Oct. 16, 1973.

18. Montessori frequently spoke about the interior Teacher in her writings. Among others, see *La Mente Del Bambino* (Milan: Garzanti, 1970), p. 7 and *La Formazione dell'Uomo* (Milan: Garzanti, 1970), p. 64. (Translator's note: This phrase is translated by Claude A. Claremont as "the inward teacher" in *The Absorbent Mind* (India: Kalakshetra Publications, 1984), p. 7. Sofia Cavalletti capitalizes the word Teacher; thus I have retained her usage because she is referring explicitly to God. The other Montessori book referred to here is *The Formation of Man*.)

19. Maria Montessori, *Autoeducazione* (Milan: Garzanti, 1970), 83. (Translator's note: See note 3 above.)

20. Franz Marc, *L'indivisibile bellezza* (Milan: Il Saggiatore, 1959), p. 43.

21. Gerhard von Rad, *Thèologie del'Ancien Testament* (Génève, 4th ed.) Volume I, p. 268–277 and *passim*; Volume II, passim. (*Old Testament Theology: The Theology of Israel's Historical Traditions*, I and II).

22. Salvatore Natoli, *L'esperienza del dolore: Le forme del patire nella cultura occidentale* (Feltrinelli, 1999), p. 144.

23. Translator's note: This phrase is also the title of a book by Abraham Joshua Heschel, *God In Search of Man.*

24. Pontificia Commissio Biblica, *Il Popolo Ebraico e le sue Scritture nella Bibbia Cristiana,* No. 37–42 (Libreria Editrice Vaticana, 1991).

25. Translator's note: From the Eucharistic liturgy.

26. See Cipriano Vagaggini, *Il Senso Teologico Della Liturgia: Saggio di liturgia teologica generale*, 4th ed. (Rome: Edizioni Paoline, 1965).

27. Jean Piaget, *Le Dévelopement de la Notion de Temps Chez L'Enfant*, 2nd ed, (Paris: Presses universitaires de France, 1981). (*The Child's Conception of Time*)

28. *Ibid.*, p. 82.

29. Hans Jonas, *Tra Il Nulla e L'Eternità* (Ferrara: Gallio, 1992), p. 81.

30. Giovanni Garbini, *Storia e Ideologia Nell' Antico Israele* (Brescia: Paideia, 1986).

31. André Neher, *L'Existence Juive: solitude et affrontements* (Paris: Seuil, 1962), p. 27ff.

32. Claude Tresmontant, *La Doctrine Morale Des Prophètes d'Israël* (Paris: Seuil, 1958), p. 181.

33. Translator's note: Although Sofia Cavalletti does not mention it in the text, I have taken the liberty of naming this heading as "The History of the Kingdom of God," to identify the name of the theme and the "material" she describes.

34. Bernard Häring, *La Loi Du Christ: théologie morale à l'intention des prêtes et des laïcs,* vol. 1 (Paris: Descléè, 1964), p. 331ff.

35. Translator's note: This rendering of stanza 23 is from *The Poems of St. John of the Cross, A Bilingual Edition,* trans. John Frederick Nims (Chicago: The University of Chicago Press, 1979), p. 11.

36. Translator's note: *Parenesis*: moral exhortation. Readers who are interested in this subject are referred to Sofia Cavalletti's two earlier works: *The Religious Potential of the*

Children, Volume I: Chapter 9, Moral Formation, p. 151–57; and *The Religious Potential of the Children, Volume II:* Chapters 12 and 13, Moral Life and Liturgy, p. 97–122.

37. The presentation of the Catechesis of the Good Shepherd in these pages is a brief synthesis of two books by Sofia Cavalletti, *Il Potenziale Religioso Del Bambino*, 3rd ed (Rome: Città Nuova, 1979); *Il Potenziale Religioso tra I 6–12 anni: Descrizione di un'Esperienza* (Rome: Città Nuova, 1996). These works are available in English: *The Religious Potential of the Child: Experiencing Scripture and Liturgy with Young Children* (Chicago: Liturgy Training Publications, 1992); *The Religious Potential of the Child 6 to 12 Years Old: A Description of an Experience* (Chicago: Liturgy Training Publications, 2002). In German: *Das Religioese Potential des Kindes* (Herder, Freiburg, Gasel, Wien, 1993) (translation not always faithful). In Spanish: *El Potencial Religioso del Niño* (Porrua, 1987); *El Potencial Religioso del Niño entre los 6 y los 12 Annos* (Porrua). In Portuguese: *Potencial Religioso da Criança* (Ed. Lodola, San Paulo, 1985). In Polish: *Basel Potencjal Duchowy Dziecka* (WAM, Cracovia, 2001); and in Korean.

Chapter Five

My Readings

Translator's Note:

Originally titled "My Books," this essay was Sofia's response to a request from a dear niece asking her to write about the "fundamental books" in her life. It was written in 2003. In 2008 Sofia returned to this work, made an addendum, and changed the title to "My Readings," but continued it as a personal letter to her niece, as her closing salutation shows.

Most often Sofia was insistent on "staying out of sight," so to speak, for the sake of more truly serving the relationship between God and children in particular. In that sense, she followed her own counsel to catechists about "hiding," as it were, behind the Christian message (see chapter 4). Therefore, this first-person account is a rarity among her writings.

In preparing this volume, I received a message from one of the first readers of this chapter who noted its value, especially for those who never met Sofia in person:

> This essay will be an invaluable resource for understanding Sofia's formation and development as a theologian, catechist, and wise guide for so many. I recognize that she has not wanted attention focused on her, yet this will point to what engaged her heart, as well as her mind, and hence, it will take its readers beyond the person to the message.

Two details in regard to the format and translation of this chapter: In the original, all the bibliographic information was embedded in the letter itself. For the purpose of facilitating an uninterrupted flow for the reader, I have placed all this material into endnotes, except for the titles of the books she addresses.

Here, as elsewhere in her writings, Sofia often capitalized the first letter of words which ordinarily would not be capitalized in English or even whole words (for example, ONE God). She did this for emphasis, and to draw attention to the special meaning or person represented by such terms. For this reason they have been retained here.

(Editor's note: For any book that is available in English, the English title is given; for all others, the title remains the same as the original.)

My dear niece,

You asked me to point out for you the fundamental books of my life. It is not easy for me to remember them. For sure I will forget many, but I will try to do it. First of all, though, I want to thank you for asking me to undertake this little work, because it has stirred peaceful memories, enabling me to meet anew the persons who have helped me greatly and whom I consider a gift to have been able to meet.

Certainly, the fundamental book for me has been the Bible, although I began to read the Old Testament at around twenty years of age, perhaps even later. I believe I refound an orientation within me which, I think, had been forming almost without my knowing, and has become constitutive of my person. It is not easy for me to explain, yet I believe I can speak of a sense of concreteness, of solidity, which is due, I believe, both to the content and the language of the Bible. God is frequently addressed in the Bible with names such as "rock," "shield," and "fortress," in the sense of "stronghold," as is seen at the start of Psalm 18. These are terms that exclude any evanescent devotionalism, as well as any intellectual theologizing, into which I would easily have fallen. All this has happened very gradually, and I became aware of it only when this orientation was surely already within me for some time.

I can say the same with regard to what I have been taught by little children. Although they are not "books," they certainly are teachers, and so I cannot leave them out of this writing. Little children are teachers without knowing that they are. They have no academic status, and precisely because of this their action has all the more impact. Their influence on me has also been gradual and profound, which I became aware of after the fact (*post eventum*).

Sofia at her desk. Photo by Patricia Coulter.

Both the Bible and little children led me to find values within myself that clearly were given to me as gift. This was something that I had not sought, that I had never asked for, nor even wished for, and in which I had to acknowledge the total gratuitousness of gift; it was something that was not the result of conscious effort, and for which I cannot be other than infinitely grateful.

For the Bible I had a master-teacher, Eugenio Zolli, from whom I learned directly and who opened to me a new way of reading the Bible. In the Catholic world of that time, the Bible had become somewhat relegated to the church sacristy.

But with Zolli, the Bible began to open totally new horizons for me. I came to discover a profundity and multiplicity of meanings in the Bible that I had never imagined. I came to realize the enormous value of the Old Testament, not only in relation to the New Testament, but in itself. I came to recognize that, between what we call the Old and New Testaments, there is not a "solution of continuity," as it has been called, because in both Testaments it is always the ONE God who is speaking and acting, in different times and situations.

I came to discover what Augustine calls the "golden thread"; that is, the constant presence of God, of God's plan, in which all the events are linked together, one to the other, in their movement forward to the fullness that all are looking toward.

I spent many hours working with Zolli and, for me, his teaching came from these live encounters with him, much more than from his writings. Among his many books, I point out particularly *The Nazarene: Studies in New Testament Exegesis*[1] (a collection of wise interpretations, especially of New Testament passages, which constitute the crux of interpretation (*crux interpretum*)).

And then there are his *Note Esegetiche*[2] published in various Italian and foreign scientific reviews, and most of all in *Biblica* from the Pontifical Biblical Institute in Rome. I wrote a synthesis of his *Notes* on the occasion of the twenty-fifth anniversary of his death: "In Memoria di Eugenio Zolli."[3] I saw the "birth" of some of his *Notes,* and in this way I learned how to approach a text with the rigorous method of research.

Other writings in the biblical field that have been important to me are those I would define as "obstinate" readings from interpretive texts in the Judaic tradition, which are called midrash. I call these "obstinate readings" because at that time not even the library of the Biblical Institute (Instituto Biblico) had many translations of them. Now it is easy to find translations and in inexpensive editions, too; Citta Nuova and Dehoniane have published many.

It was not easy for me to understand everything, but I did not give up and went ahead all the same. I believe I did well because along the way I was absorbing the midrashic method. That method, which sets aside the historical-critical method, juxtaposes text with text, without focusing on their eventual dating or with their literary genre.

The midrashic method takes seriously the fact that the Bible is ONE book, in which there is always the ONE God, who makes himself known and whose words resound in "seventy languages." The midrashic method, in proposing unexpected juxtapositions, amplifies illimitably the interpretive horizon. I do not remember if these readings preceded or followed the death of Zolli, my master-teacher; Zolli's way of approaching the Bible, however, prepared me to receive these readings.

So as not to become insulated, because by that time in my life mornings spent in the library were past history (since I had reached 80 years of age), I read a series of books dedicated to the current state of biblical studies.

Consigning the historical-critical method to second place, I discovered many methods of reading [the Bible] that were in tune with the new currents of scholarship (structuralism, narrative, etc.) and in which it was not easy to get one's bearings. I note especially the scholars of the Biblical Institute which I read with interest and benefit: Jean-Louis Ska's *Introduction to Reading the Pentateuch*[4] and *Our Fathers Have Told Us: Introduction to the Analysis of Hebrew Narratives on Narrative Theology*,[5] as well as *Methodologia dell'Antico Testamento*,[6] edited by H. Simian Yofre, and *Breve Storia del'Esegesi Biblica*,[7] by Pierre Gilbert from the Institut Catholique in Lyons.

Of course, these books from the best scholars in the biblical field are important and very useful. Nevertheless, they are insufficient to help give that lift to one's wings, which is capable of placing the person who is reading in a stance of listening to a Word, a Word which has no limits and yet is addressed personally to each individual.

Interesting studies are being done by the Community of Montevegli founded by Giuseppe Dossetti, an Italian politician. After he left politics, he became a monk and established his monastic community. It is located in a center in Israel and that was where I first met Dossetti, when I participated in their Sunday morning liturgy in Jerusalem, near the Mount of Olives. What a beautiful experience! In their celebrations the texts are read in their original languages. The community is serious about living the inseparable unity between Bible and liturgy.

Dossetti's *Per una "Chiesa Eucaristica,"* a compilation of his 1965 lectures, with commentary and editing by G. Alberigo and G. Ruggeri, is important for going deeply into the complexity of his work.[8] It is a retrospective of what Dossetti has done for the "paideia" (education) of the Catholic Church, which, he says "needs to recognize itself as culturally poor, in surrendering security based on a system of rationality, in order to entrust itself to the absolute richness of the sacred text."

The "poverty" Dossetti desires for the Church is definitely not ignorance. Rather, it is the poverty of the one who feels disarmed in facing the Mystery, which is so much greater than oneself; it is the "poverty" of the one who feels increasingly smaller—and happier!—as one gradually enters into the Mystery. This kind of poverty is the base upon which the center of theological studies in Bologna, inspired by Dossetti, was founded.

If it is permissible to compare little things with great things (*Si parva licet componere magnis*), I would say that it is upon this kind of poverty that the Catechesis of the Good Shepherd, which has been defined as the ABCs of Christianity, is founded.

The monks of Dossetti's community are dedicated in a particular way to Jewish-Christian dialogue and to an ever-deepening study of the Jewish tradition. Some of their publications that I have studied are: *Le Scritture ai Tempi di Gesū* by S. P. Carbone-G.Rizzi[9] and *Osea, Lettura Ebraica, Greca e Aramaica* by Umberto Neri and G. Rizzi,[10] a book dedicated to the interaction among the three traditions current in the earliest centuries of Christianity. Umberto Neri, a monk of Dossetti's community, wrote another book, *La Crisi Biblica dell'Età Moderna,*[11] that is very helpful in situating oneself.

A very interesting book, compiled by Neri with a beautiful introduction by Dossetti, is *Genesi.*[12] This work goes through the Book of Genesis verse by verse, adding various interpretations, as in the "grand tradition" of reading scripture. It begins with Targum, the Aramaic translation (every translation is also an interpretation), and continues up to recent scholars like von Rad. The project is very vast. Unhappily, Umberto Neri has died, but other books in this series have come out: one volume contains the books of Joel, Amos, and Obadiah, and another is on the Letter to the Ephesians.[13]

As you know, the parables hold a very important place in the Catechesis of the Good Shepherd. On this point, various books of Paul Ricoeur have been enlightening: *Biblical Hermeneutics,*[14] *Ermeneutica Filosofica ed Ermeneutica Biblica,*[15] and *L'Herménétique Biblique.*[16] Some other books on this theme are Norman Perrin, *Jesus and the Language of the Kingdom*;[17] Otto Via, *The Parables*[18]; Elian Cuvillier, *Le Concept de Parabole dans Le Second Evangile*.[19] On the other hand, the well-known book by Joachim Jeremias on the parables disappointed me.

Paul Ricoeur helped me greatly in understanding the workings of the conscience with his book, *Finitude et Culpabilité*.[20] And, obviously, Saint Augustine's work *On the Teacher*.[21] Augustine's saying "I can never teach" (*Numquam possum docere*) has been like a guiding light in my work.

To help clarify the historical orientation of the Catechesis of the Good Shepherd, I leaned on Paul Ricoeur, *History and Truth*[22], and on Pierre Grélot, *Le Sens Chrétien de l'Ancien Testament*.[23] Among biblical theologians, I must mention the two-volume work by Gerhard von Rad, *Old Testament Theology*.[24] Jean Daniélou's *Sacramentum Futuri*[25] helped me enter into typology.

My study with Zolli was certainly the determining factor with respect to my interest in Jewish-Christian dialogue. And so I joined the Italian Ecumenical Commission (CEI), in the course of which I had most interesting meetings with Maria Vingiani, whom I consider to be the "mother" of ecumenism in Italy. Maria founded the Secretariat of Ecumenical Activities (SAE) and wove an extensive net of relationships among other Christian communities and especially with Judaism, which Maria deemed, rightly, the point of departure for all ecumenism.

The encounters with Maria helped me become aware of how much we owe to Judaism, not only because it is "the root that carries us," but also because modern Judaism teaches us to refind in our own faith certain realities which, although they were always present, stayed in the shadows and no longer fed our lives as believers.

Among these realities, what seems to me to be of greatest importance is the messianic tension, to be conscious that we too are a people in waiting, and that, therefore, the foundational virtue also for us is **hope**, the stretching toward a completion. Everything is completed in the person of Jesus, yet, for now, it is fulfilled only in him; whereas the plan of God is to establish a "kingdom," a plan to attain the moment in history when "God will be all in all" (1 Corinthians 15:28). This is the object of our waiting, of our hope.

Staying with the subject of Jewish-Christian dialogue, the writings of Francesco Rossi de Gasperis have been significant. He is a Jesuit, whom I also first met in Jerusalem and then saw again later in Rome. His article, "Israele e la Radice Santa della Nostra Fede,"[26] made me especially aware of the importance, for our faith, of the earliest Christian generations. These first generations were certainly very limited in terms of numbers, "However," says de Gasperis, "we are dealing with a minority *qualitatively powerful and culturally influential as to preside,* as Jacob Jervel basically asserts, *authoritatively and effectively over the redaction of not only one or another Christian writing, but over the entire New Testament.*"

And this opens up a subject of extreme importance: namely, that there was a Church, one that preceded the great councils (The Council of Nicea, 325: the consubstantiality of the Father and the Son (*omousios*); the Council of Constantinople, 381: the "proceeding" of the Spirit from the Father and the Son (the well-known *Filioque*); the Council of Ephesus, 431: the divine motherhood of Mary; the Council of Chalcedon 451: the two natures in Christ). From these points derive all the subsequent theological speculation. Those very first generations of Christians overlooked all such speculation, and they were assuredly Christian generations. Such a fact as this cannot but open new horizons, not only with regard to Christian-Jewish relations, but also for ecumenism among Christian churches as well.

This subject is very dear to Rossi de Gasperis, one which he has treated in many works. I note particularly *Cominciando da Gerusalemme,* in which a great number of his very interesting studies are collected. The title is already programmatic in itself: Rossi de Gasperis affirms that the Christian Church does not begin in Rome but in Jerusalem; Jerusalem is the Mother Church.

With respect to this point of view, it is extremely interesting to read what he says in the chapter of this book about the fermentation happening in the Jewish Christian community present at that time in Israel, and not only in Israel. He defines these "ferments as neither pre-Nicene, nor pre-Ephesian, nor pre-Chalcedonian" but as *"extra-Nicene, extra-Ephesian, extra-Chalcedonian."* That is, he is speaking about a new Judeo-Christianity, which was emerging on the part of the believers in Jesus, who "did not feel obligated to retrace all the steps in the problematic confrontation between faith and culture, which certain churches had to contend with in other historical periods and in different cultural contexts."[27]

Even the Councils are necessarily conditioned by the culture of the time in which they were held, in response to the needs of a particular time and in a specific culture. I am very passionate about this subject because—without being aware of it—I was coming across it in my work with the children. Young children know nothing of all the investigations and theological subtleties of ancient councils or university scholars. Nonetheless, children reach a very deep level of Christian knowledge (and this is documented by the *theological drawings* they are capable of doing), knowledge that is *theological* but not in the sense of university theology.

According to Evagrius Ponticus, a teacher in the Oriental church, the theologian is "the one who *knows how to pray*." We are speaking about knowledge that is *essential* for the Christian faith, which is based on the solid foundation of the biblical-liturgical sources; if we were to present children with subtle arguments and complicated theology, they would understand nothing.

You can easily see how delicate this subject is and also how important it is in relation to a rediscovery of an *essential* theology, capable of nourishing a solid life of faith in those "little ones" to whom the Father reveals "these things" (what will "these things" be? eschatological realities perhaps?) which instead are hidden to "the wise and the intelligent" (Matthew 11:25; Luke 10:21). Fundamentally—it would seem—it is about a different way of being Christians.

In addition, this subject is most interesting from an ecumenical perspective in terms of relations with other sister Churches and from the missionary point of view. If the Catechesis of the Good Shepherd were based on doctrine of the university kind, it certainly would not have the reception it has with the Totonac people (of the Sierra di Puebla in Mexico), or with the indigenous people of Panama and other Latin American countries, or with the Zulu in South Africa. And it would not have expanded in the widespread way it has to Churches of different traditions.

Maria Christlieb, a Mexican catechist of the Good Shepherd, who died prematurely, wrote about such an experience in her diary, *Dios y el Nino se Entienden*. She told the story about the day she was to speak about the words of Jesus at the Last Supper during a course for adults, attended by persons from different denominations. Maria did not use terms such as "transubstantiation" or similar types of words, and she writes:

> Any interpretation of ours, other than what Christ said, would have separated us immediately. Offering only the pure proclamation that the Shepherd invites us with his Word joined us together deeply. Presenting the sources in their essentiality and in a completely objective form united us deeply. There was a common language. There was the essential. We all listened to it and we all fell in love with it.[28]

And now we come to the liturgy.

I refound the Bible in the liturgy, but unencumbered by any intellectual or scientific overlay, a direction in which the prevailing historical-critical method threatened to take me, even though the teaching of Zolli had repositioned me. Through the liturgy I refound the Bible, but more alive in the celebration. Gradually I came to understand that the Bible and the liturgy form one whole: the liturgy celebrates what the Bible recounts.

If we did not have the Bible, the liturgy would not have the concrete historical foundation to support it. If we did not have the liturgy, biblical history would be a most beautiful and interesting account, yet far distant from those who lived those events.

The study of the Jewish Passover liturgy (*haggadah* or *seder*) has been extremely important for me. This study led me to understand that the liturgy is always *memorial*: through the liturgy the great events of the history of salvation are made present *here* and *now, for me*. That is, those very events in which we were not present, and about which, if we did not have the memorial, we would have to say: "How unfortunate! I wasn't there; I was born too late. I have lost something of utmost importance."

A classic work on the memorial is Max Thurian's *The Eucharistic Memorial*.²⁹ Max Thurian is a cofounder of the Taizé community; he later entered the Catholic Church.

As for my studies in liturgy, my formation was mostly by means of books. For me, the fundamental one was Cipriano Vagaggini's *Theological Dimension of the Liturgy*, first published 1957 and in other subsequent editions.³⁰ Vagaggini was a Benedictine monk at Saint Anselm's, and a great architect of the Second Vatican Council's Constitution on Liturgy (*Sacrosanctum Concilium*).

At the start of my work in the Catechesis, I turned to him for advice about the program I had drafted for the course for adults. And he also helped me with the first publications that we worked on with the Pauline publishers. He spent the last part of his life as a hermit with the Camaldolese in Tuscany.

He affirmed that the liturgy, which had been downgraded to "a science of rubrics," is a most important source of theology; it is a source that does not speak the language of abstract theology, but rather by signs—the universal, concrete language that is grasped not only with the mind, but with the eyes, by looking, touching. A synthesis of Vagaggini's thought is found in *Liturgia e Pensiero Teologico*.³¹ It contains the introductory address he gave at the inauguration of the Pontifical Liturgical Institute of St. Anselm.

A most beautiful book by Vagaggini is called *Caro Salutis est Cardo: Corporeità Eucharistica e Liturgia*.³² In this book he maintains that inasmuch as liturgy is a complex of sensible signs it has the closest possible bond to the Incarnation.

A liturgist once said to me that I would have everything I needed in Vagaggini's book and the four volumes of Mario Righetti's *Storia della Liturgia*, which contains a wealth of information on the history of the rites.³³

Also valuable to me were the many conversations I had on the liturgy with Tommaso Luigi Federici, whom I met at Sapienza University. He, too, was a student of Professor Zolli. Later he became a passionate liturgist and taught at St. Anselm's and for The Society for the Propagation of the Faith (*Propaganda Fide*). His books, however, are very laborious.

At a conference some time later, I met Enrico Mazza, a liturgical historian; after that, I read many of his books with much enjoyment (but not all his articles, which are in the hundreds). I note especially his *Mystagogy: A Theology of Liturgy in the Patristic Age.*[34]

He confirmed for me—very authoritatively—that typology (a method of reading the history in the Bible, by considering its various events in the light of the globality of history itself, which we had already been doing with the children) is a theology composed of facts rather than words alone.

Thus typology is, just as it had seemed to me, a theology for "little ones," and not only in the chronological sense. Mazza helped me to become more conscious that liturgical acts are *"events which carry forward the history of salvation."* Before this I had already read some works by the great mystagogues of the fourth century, such as Ambrose, Cyril of Jerusalem, and John Chrysostom; I had not read Gregory of Mopsuestia. They had familiarized me with the language of signs and I was enamored by it. But I came to realize that there was (and there is!) still more to discover.

Two other works by Enrico Mazza I want to point out are *Le Odierne Preghiere Eucharistiche*[35] and *Continuità e Discontinuità.*[36] A great multivolume work on the liturgy is *Anàmnesis.* I only have a few of the volumes. One volume is on the historical panorama of the liturgy.[37] The other one is on the Eucharist, in which there is a lengthy contribution by Salvatore Marsili, a Benedictine monk at St. Anselm's, whom I knew.

For moral theology my master-teacher was Father Dalmazio Mongillo, OP I cannot give you a bibliography of his works. His charism was to be a great communicator of the spoken word; unfortunately, however, the same cannot be said of his communication by means of the written word. I have a certain number of cassette recordings of him, which I regard as very precious.

I will cite just one example of his way of expressing himself, which I think I told you about: the difference between "the morality of the True Vine" and "the morality of Christmas tree." The latter may appear very beautiful and all a-glitter, but what captures the eye is totally artificial. Everything comes from the outside, although the tree itself is dead. The fruits of the True Vine come from the sap that courses through its branches, which is the life of the risen Christ communicated to us.

What made me "discover" the measure of Father Dalmazio was this phrase that came at the end of what was (I think) our first meeting: "What have we done to Christianity! An amassing of norms! When it is to enjoy a Person." This encounter led me to attend his weekly course at the Angelicum for a number of semesters; the audiotapes I mentioned come from those seminars. His two-hour seminar on Monday morning gave me enough nourishment to last for the whole week.

The orientation of the moral formation in the Catechesis of the Good Shepherd came from the felicitous meeting between the positive vision of the moral life from Father Dalmazio and the capacity of children to fall in love. The doing of good and the obedience to norms come only in the second moment. The first is the moment of falling in love; it is the attraction to the light. And it is in looking at the light that the norms reveal the nature of their being as gift, that is, as guides toward what is attracting us. If we focus on the negative, we will stay stuck in the negative and not get out of it.

Speaking about gifts, although my readings on the subject have been rather few, I want to highlight this theme because gift—gratuitousness—is a great dynamism in the world. I came to the famous study by Marcel Mauss on this subject through Lévi-Strauss's work, *Introduction to the Work of Marcel Mauss*.[38] It is a work of anthropology and very capable of generating interest on this theme. I had already read Oscar Battaglia's *La Teologia del Dono* on the theme of "gift."[39] It is a simple, clear, and honest book.

Perhaps what struck me most was the book by J.T. Godbout, *Lo Spirito del Dono*.[40] The author, a sociologist, presents a positive vision of our world, in which, as he demonstrates, the spirit of gift is very present. Another book by the same author is *Le Language du Don;* an expanded edition is *Il Linguaggio del Dono*.[41] I have not read Jean Duvignaud's *Le Don du Rien*, but it might be worth looking at.[42]

A thinker who has definitely had a great importance in my life is Teilhard de Chardin. My brother Marcello introduced me to Teilhard de Chardin, and I have read a great many of his works, which have helped me to leave behind that nineteenth-century atmosphere (or pre-Vatican II in any case) that still predominated then.

I think the 1800s were a very negative period for the Church, because instead of teaching us that faith is a "wager," a challenge, as Pascal said—in which the only certainty is God, whose Person is assuredly fascinating, yet hardly easy to comprehend—it sought certainties (up to the point of infallibility) and thereby restricted the horizons. "God's foolishness is wiser than human wisdom" (1 Corinthians 1:25) had been forgotten.

With Teilhard, the windows opened for me and a different air started to circulate. His cosmic vision captivated me and it seemed to me to be in perfect accord with the Bible, although this vision did not spare him a series of problems. I am very appreciative that your father introduced me to him, in spite of the fact that he found Teilhard's thought to be lacking as regards the problem of evil.

Among my readings I should name many fairy tales too. But my nieces and nephews can give you a more updated and expanded bibliography on this subject.

> Thank you for your attentiveness.
> An embrace, Sofia
> April 4, 2003, Rome

Addendum

The books of Joseph Moingt have been really important and, I would say, very reassuring in some way. First, I read his work *Dieu Qui Vient à L'homme* (2002), a most welcome Christmas present received that same year.[43] And then I read the volume that preceded it, *L'Homme Qui Venait de Dieu* (1993).[44] I put off reading it awhile, because I am generally diffident about theologians, considering that they complicate matters. This is definitely not the case with Moingt. Despite the lofty level and the great quantity of his writing, his ideas are extremely clear and he expounds them clearly. Once I began reading his works, this has meant I went on devouring them.

Moingt says two things which mutually complete each other. The first is that religions bring along with them two things through the course of centuries and millennia. One is what he calls "the well-known God" ("bien-connu de Dieu"), that is, those things that all religions affirm, even if in different forms; for example, the omnipotence of God.

Moingt says that what has been called "the death of God" is the dissolution of "the well-known God"; this is particularly the case with omnipotence, which had led to what Bonhoeffer named the "stop-gap God," as he says in *Resistenza e Resa*.[45] This certainly is a distorted and reductionist idea of God, the result of which was that prayer had become only about petition. And there is so much else to prayer.

The omnipotence of God is a theme one meets in the Jewish philosopher Hans Jonas, who wrote *Le Concept de Dieu après Auschwitz* (which I read in its Italian translation, *Il Melangolo*).[46] It is in relation to this aspect of Moingt's theology that I consider reading his works as "reassuring." The expression "God is dead" is indeed alarming, but it needs to be understood in the manner he says—and I think justly—"It's about time!" Perhaps we will come to know from God step by step what is necessary for us to know in the age in which we live.

And now to his second point: inculturation. Christianity developed in a Hellenistic environment and thus was founded on a base of thought which is not present-day thinking. Our present-day thought has gone from interest in "being" (ousia) to historicity, from the pre-earthly, pre-existent Christ, to the Christ of history and in history.

An incarnate God, a God "in history," is a God—if it is possible to say so—who "gets one's hands dirty," who strips himself of his omnipotence, who shares in our condition even up to the point of death. And this is the aspect of God that our age needs.

Here is the place where the two points in Moingt's thinking meet and complete one another. Insofar as God was spoken of as eternal, immutable, impassive, then to speak of his "death" could sound like absolute blasphemy. When God, in Christ, immersed himself in the human situation—and this is the newness of Christianity—we have a God who is close to us.

And what is arresting is that, in the human life situation of his Son, God refinds omnipotence. Omnipotence "hides itself" in death and then, from that moment of darkness, it is manifested in the victory over death, in the Resurrection.

Sofia and Father Dalmazio Mongillo, during his conference at the first international gathering of the Catechesis of the Good Shepherd, Rome, 1993. (Photographer unknown)

This seems to me to be consonant with the whole message that Jesus Christ brings us, and that we encounter, for instance, in his comparing the Kingdom of God to the mustard seed, to the yeast. These parables are unfathomable, and they try to prepare our eyes to search for God, not in what is imposing or in what makes noise; instead, it is to seek God in what is "little."

In fact, when we read that Jesus "exulted in the Holy Spirit"—the only time recorded in his earthly life—it is when he says "I thank you, Father, because you have hidden these things from the wise and the intelligent and have revealed them to infants" (Luke 10:21ff.; Matthew 11:25 ff.). Jesus has been sent to "evangelize the poor" (Luke 4). The poor and the little are one single category.

Before closing, I would like to point out the seventy-page Prologue called "La Rumeur de Jésus" that Moingt wrote to the first volume of his book I mentioned (published in 1993). "Rumeur" is a word I do not know how to translate into Italian with just one word. The author explains it as "news from an uncontrolled source, which spreads from mouth to ear."[47] In Italian it could be translated as "voice that runs." The author says that "rumor" is a very complicated thing, and that he did not wish to lose himself in endless historical research, but "to position oneself at the level of listening to the living account": what was told about Jesus and what can still be told.

In that sense, he says, Jesus did not enter into history when he was born, but on the day after his Death, through what was told about him and the questions the people asked about him.

If we think of the little world of the land of Israel at the time of Jesus, communication was facilitated precisely by its small dimensions. And because travel from one place to another was done on foot in that country, it gave plenty of time to comment on the happenings of the day and about the rabbi, who preached in parables and worked miracles.

The matter becomes much more impassioned when word starts to spread that many saw Jesus after his Death, and talk begins about his Resurrection. We remember that the Pharisees, the most numerous religious current during the time of Jesus, professed faith in resurrection.

It is from these elements that the "rumor" about Jesus originated and progressed throughout the decades following the Gospels, and the preaching of the ancient Church depends on them. Starting from this vital nucleus—"The One who had been condemned and put to death whom God has raised" (Acts: 2:23–24ff.)—it is later discovered how Jesus is connected with the Old Testament prophecies, and this moves forward toward eschatology.

These brief references help us to understand the originality of Moingt's approach and his importance. The pages I refer to are very dense and very rich, which I certainly do not claim to synthesize in these few words. I only wish to draw attention to his writings.

Endnotes

1. Eugenio Zolli, *Il Nazareno* (Istituto delle Edizioni Accademiche, Udine, 1938). *The Nazarene: Studies in New Testament Exegesis* (New Hope, KY: St. Martin de Porres Lay Dominican Community, 1999).

2. Eugenio Zolli, *Note Esegetiche* (Firenze: Tipografia Enrico Ariani, 1933).

3. Sofia Cavalletti, *Rivista Biblica Italiana* (1983), pp. 69–92.

4. Jean-Louis Ska, *Introduzione alla lettura del Pentateuco* (Rome: Edizioni Dehoniane, 2000). *Introduction to Reading the Penteteuch* (Winona Lake, IN: Eisenbrauns, 2006).

5. Jean-Louis Ska, SJ, *Our Fathers Have Told Us* (Rome: Biblical Institute Press, 1990).

6. H. Simian Yofre (ed), *Methodologia dell'Antico Testamento* (Bologne: EDB, 1994).

7. Pierre Gilbert, *Breve Storia del'Esegesi Biblica* (Queriniana, 1995).

8. Giuseppe Dossetti, *Per una "Chiesa eucaristica,"* ed. G. Alberigo and G. Ruggeri (Bologna: Società editrice il Mulino, 2002).

9. S. P. Carbone-G. Rizzi, *Le Scritture ai Tempi di Gesū* (Bologna: Dehoniane, 1992).

10. Umberto Neri-G. Rizzi, *Osea, Lettura Ebraica, Greca e Aramaica* (Bologna: EDB, 1992).

11. Umberto Neri, *La Crisi Biblica dell'Età Moderna* (Bologna: EDB, 1966).

12. Umberto Neri, *Genesi* (Torino: Gribauti, 1986).

13. Gioele, *Amos e Abdia; Efesini* (Torino: Gribauti).

14. Paul Ricoeur, *Biblical Hermeneutics* (Society of Biblical Literature, 1975).

15. Paul Ricoeur, *Ermeneutica Filosofica ed Ermeneutica Biblica* (Paideia, 1977).

16. Paul Ricoeur, *L'Herménétique Biblique* (Cerf, Paris, 2001).

17. Norman Perrin, *Jesus and the Language of the Kingdom* (Philadelphia, 1976).

18. Otto Via, *The Parables* (Philadelphia, 1967).

19. Evan Cuvillier, *Le Concept de PARABOLE dans Le Second Evangile* (Paris: Gabalda, 1993).

20. Paul Ricoeur, *Finitude et Culpabilité* (Paris: Aubier Montaigne, 1960). (Translator's note: This book is published in English as *Fallible Man*, trans. Charles A. Kelbely (New York: Fordham University Press, 1986).)

21. Saint Augustine, *De Magistro* (*On The Teacher*).

22. Paul Ricoeur, *Histoire et Verité* (Paris: Seuil, 1955). *History and Truth*, trans. Charles A. Kelbley (Evanston: Northwestern University Press, 1965 (1955)).

23. Pierre Grélot, *Le Sens Chrétien de l'Ancien Testament* (Paris: Desclée, 1962).

24. Gerhard von Rad, *Old Testament Theology,* vols. I and II (New York: Harper, 1963, 1967).

25. Jean Daniélou, *Sacramentum Futuri* (Paris: Beauchesne, 1950).

26. Francesco Rossi de Gasperis, "Israele e la radice santa della nostra fede," *Rassegna di Teologia* 21 (1980), 1–15; 116–129.

27. Francesco Rossi De Gasperis, *Cominciando da Gerusalemme (Lc 24, 47): la sorgente della fede e dell'esistenza Cristiana* (Piemme: Casale Monferrato, 1994). See chapter "Un nuovo giudeocristianesimo e la sua possibile rilevanza ecclesiale". (Translator's note: The quote is taken from p. 151.)

28. Maria Christlieb, *Dios y el nino se entienden* (Mexico, 2002), p. 180. (Translator's note: *God and The Child Understand Each Other*.)

29. Max Thurian, *L'Eucharistie* (Delachaux et Niestlé, 1963). *The Eucharistic Memorial* (Richmond: John Knox Press, 1963).

30. Cipriano Vagaggini, *Il Senso Teologico della Liturgia* (Paoline, 1957). *Theological Dimensions of the Liturgy* (Collegeville, MN: Liturgical Press, 1959).

31. Cipriano Vagaggini, *Liturgia e Pensiero Teologico* (Rome: Pontificio Ateneo Anselmiano, 1961).

32. Cipriano Vagaggini, *Caro Salutis est Cardo: Corporeità Eucharistica e Liturgia* (Desclée de Brower 1966). *The Flesh: Instrument of Salvation: A Theology of the Human Body*, (New York: Society of St. Paul, 1969.)

33. Mario Righetti, *Storia Della Liturgia* (Milan: Ancora, 1950–59).

34. Enrico Mazza, *La Mistagogia, Una Teologia della Liturgia in Epoca Patristica* (Liturgiche, 1988). *Mystagogy: A Thelogy of Liturgy in the Patristic Age* (New York: Pueblo, 1989).

35. Enrico Mazza, *Le Odierne Preghiere Eucharistiche* (Rome: EDB, 1984).

36. Enrico Mazza, *Continuità e Discontinuità: Concezioni Medievali dell'Eucharistia a Aonfronto con la Tradizione dei Padri a della Liturgia* (Liturgiche, 2001).

37. *Anàmnesis Vol. 1: La Liturgia, Momento nella Storia della Salvezza*. B. Neunheuser, S. Marsili, M. Augé, R. Civil (Marietti, 1974).

38. Claude Lévi-Strauss: *Introduzione a Marcel Mauss: Teoria Generale della Magia* (Einaudi, 1965). *Introduction to the Work of Marcel Mauss* (London: Routledge and Kegan Paul, 1987)

39. Oscar Battaglia, *La Teologia del Dono: Ricerca di Teologia Biblica sul Tema del Dono di Dio nel Vangelo e nella 1 Lettera di Giovanni* (Assisi: Studio Teologico "Porziuncola," 1971).

40. J.T. Godbout, *Lo Spirito del Dono* (Bollati Boringhieri, 1993).

41. J.T. Godbout, *Le Language du Don* (Fides, Montréal, 1993). Expanded edition: *Il Linguaggio del Dono* (Turin: Bollatti Boringhieri, 1998).

42. L. Duvignaud, *Le Don du Rien: Essai d'Anthropologie de la Fete* (Paris: Stock, 1977).

43. Joseph Moingt, *Dieu Qui Vient à L'homme* (Paris: Cerf, 2002),

44. Joseph Moingt, *L'Homme Qui Venait de Dieu* (Paris: Cerf, 1993).

45. Dietrich Bonhoeffer, *Resistenza e Resa* (Eberhard Bethge, Paoline, 1988). (Translator's note: See: "Letter to Eberhard Bethge, 29 May 1944," in *Letters and Papers From Prison, The Enlarged Edition*. Ed. Eberhard Bethge. Touchstone Book, New York, 1997, p. 311–312.)

46. Hans Jonas, *Le Concept de Dieu après Auschwitz* (Italian: *Il Melangolo,* 1990).

47. Joseph Moingt, *L'Homme Qui Venait de Dieu* (Paris: Cerf, 1993), p. 25.

Chapter Six

Curriculum Vitae

Translator's Note:
Short as it is, Sofia's *curriculum vitae* belongs in a chapter of its own. Its placement at the end of this book is in recognition of Sofia's preference for staying as far as possible in the background. She would insist that this book is meant to focus on God and children, not the writer. Some details are unavoidable, however, particularly for those for whom this may be an initial meeting with Sofia and her life's work.

There are two obvious points to be noted about this brief CV. The first is that Sofia clearly never intended this to be an in-depth treatment of her life and work, even up to that point. Therefore, you will notice the lack of detail about her writings, which, by 1977 alone, already numbered over 200 (articles and books, etc.). You will also see, especially in the final few lines, that Sofia makes only the briefest allusion to her work as a whole.

The second point relates to the fact that Sofia is writing this at 79 years of age. Everything is left unsaid about the following 15 years, during which she was actively involved in a breadth of activities. For instance, Sofia remained deeply engaged in the Good Shepherd catechesis right up to the time of her death. Actually, this period marks a most creative period of her life, about which I offer just two examples.

In 1996, the date of this CV, Sofia instigated and convoked, with the help of Gianna and her colleagues in Rome, the first formal gathering of catechists representing all the countries in which the Good Shepherd catechesis was then rooted. This initiative became a focus of Sofia's most avid dedication. The many such meetings of the "International Council" (*Consiglio*), over these years, were all housed in her home, and have contributed incalculably to the spread of the catechesis. Today it is present in 25 countries, on five continents.

The other example relates to her constant creative output during these ensuing years. Her works have since been translated into many languages, most recently—and to her grateful delight—in Chinese and Zulu. At the end of this book we have added a listing of both her written and audiovisual works relating specifically to the Catechesis of the Good Shepherd.

Curriculum Vitae

1936: Certification: Catechetical Instruction for Elementary School, Vicariate of Rome.

1936: Certification: French Studies, Course of Champs Elysées.

1937: Certification: Catechetical Instruction for High School, Vicariate of Rome.

1941: Certification: Proficiency in English, University of Cambridge.

1948–1952: Volunteer Assistant to Chair of Hebrew and Comparative Semitic Languages, Sapienza University, Rome.

1949: Doctoral Degree: Hebrew and Comparative Semitic Languages, Sapienza University, Rome.

1952: Specialization: Philology, Culture, and History of the Ancient Semitic Peoples, Oriental Institute, Sapienza University, Rome.

1954: Began collaboration with Gianna Gobbi, Center of the Catechesis of the Good Shepherd, Rome.

1954/8–1973/4: Taught Religion, Armando Diaz Professional Institute, Montessori Department, Via Gaeta, Rome.

1957/8–1973/4: Taught Religion, Virgil State High School, Experimental Montessori Department, Via Giulia, Rome.

1958: Published: *Uno Studio Introduttivo, al Talmud Babilonese, Trattato delle Benedizioni*, compiled by Eugenio Zolli (Ed. Laterza), pp. XI–LII. Republished 1968 (Ed. UTET) and 1992 (Ed. TEA).

1960: Collaborated in the translation of the books of Isaiah and Proverbs, in *Sacra Bibbia* (Ed. Fiorentina).

1961: Published: In collaboration with Gianna Gobbi: *Educazione Religiosa, Liturgia e Metodo Montessori* (Ed. Paoline). In 1964 in English: *Teaching Doctrine and Liturgy* (St. Paul Publications). In 1965 in Portuguese: *Educaçao Religiosa, Liturgia e Metodo Montessori* (Ed. Paolinas).

1965:   Published: In collaboration with Gianna Gobbi, *Io Sono Il Buon Pastore*. Christian doctrine for elementary children; five volumes for children and five volumes for catechists (Ed. Coletti).

1966:   Published: *Ebraismo e Spiritualità* (Ed. Studium).

1968:   Published: Introduction, translation and commentary on the Books of Ruth and Esther, in *Nuovissima Versione Della Bibbia* (Ed. Paoline). In 1976: Published: Introduction, translation and commentary on the Book of Leviticus.

1975:   Collaborated: *Dizionairo Enciclopedico di Spiritualità* (Ed. Studium).

1977:   Published: "*L'Educazione Ebraica*," in *Nuove Questioni Di Storia Della Pedagogia* (Ed. La Scuola), pp. 1–62.

1979:   Published: *El Potenziale Religioso Del Bambino* (Città Nuova Editrice); 4th ed. 1993. In 1983 in English: *The Religious Potential of the Child* (Paulist Press); republished in 1993 (Liturgy Training Publications). In 1985 in Portuguese: *Potencial religioso da çrianca* (Loyola, Sao Paolo, Brasile). In 1987 in Spanish: *Il potencial religioso del niño* (Porrua). In 1994 in German: *Das Religioese Potential des Kindes* (Herder, Wien).

1983:   Published: *Contro La Violenza, Una Donna: Il Libro di Guiditta* (Ed. ELLE DI CI).

1984:   Published: "*La Mistica Ebraica*," in *La Mistica, Fenemenologia e Riflessione Teologica* (Ed. Città Nuova), pp. 613–652.

1985:   Published: "Introduction" to E. Lévinas, *Dal Sacro Al Santo* (Ed. Città Nuova).

1989:   Published: "Preface" to P. H. Peli, *La Torah* (Ed. Marietti).

1991:   Published: *Il Giudaismo Intertestamentario* (Ed. Queriniana).

1992:   Published: "Preface" to: E. Kopciowski, *I Libri Dei Profeti e La Torah Oggi* (Ed. Marietti).

1993:   Collaborated on: *Dizionario di Spiritualità Biblico-Patristico* (Ed. Borla).

1996:   Published: *Il Potenziale Religioso tra i 6 e i 12 anni* (Ed. Città Nuova).

* Taught International courses on the Catechesis of the Good Shepherd in the USA, Canada, Mexico, Israel, Ireland, France, England, Croatia, Germany.

* Articles on biblical and postbiblical subjects in Italian and foreign reviews.

* Articles on religious education in Italian and foreign reviews.

* Member: Ecumenical Commission, Italian Episcopal Conference; Ecumenical Commission, Diocese of Rome.

* Presenter for the Multicultural Montessori Congress, held October 3, 1996.

About the Author

Translator's Note:
It may be of interest to know that Sofia wrote this for a previous book, and for this reason it is included here.

Sofia Cavalletti received her degree in Hebrew and Comparative Semitic Languages from the Sapienza University, Rome. She contributed to several editions of the Bible (Old Testament), translating Isaiah, Leviticus, Ruth, Esther, Judith, and Proverbs, and to international publications on biblical studies. Dr. Cavalletti was also a specialist in the field of ecumenism, especially the Jewish-Christian relationship.

In 1954, Sofia Cavalletti, together with Gianna Gobbi, began the Good Shepherd Center of Catechesis for children and adults in Rome. This work has spread to five continents through lectures, seminars, courses, and publications, which have been translated into many languages.

In the course of more than 55 years' experience with children age two and older, the children have revealed unexpected capacities in their relationship with the Transcendent. Children from very diverse geographical, social, and cultural environments have always responded to this relationship with a profound sense of joy. This puts them in a particular state of peace, which makes us think that this relationship satisfies a vital need within children.

Cavalletti, Sofia

The Religious Potential of the Child: Experiencing Scripture and Liturgy with Young Children (Chicago: Liturgy Training Publications, 1992).

The Religious Potential of the Child: 6 to 12 Years Old (Chicago: Liturgy Training Publications, 2002).

The History of the Kingdom of God Part I: From Creation to Parousia (Chicago: Liturgy Training Publications, forthcoming Spring 2012); a revision of *History's Golden Thread*.

The History of the Kingdom of God Part II: Liturgy and the Building of the Kingdom (Chicago: Liturgy Training Publications, forthcoming); a revision of *Living Liturgy*.

With Patricia Coulter, Gianna Gobbi, and Silvana Montanaro, *The Good Shepherd and The Child: A Joyful Journey* (Chicago: Liturgy Training Publications, 2003).

Ways to Nurture the Relationship with God. (Chicago: Liturgy Training Publications, 2010).

Catechesis of the Good Shepherd: Essential Realities (Chicago: Liturgy Training Publications, 2004).

Remember the Lord Your God: A History of the Jewish People, (Timeline (scroll), Book for Adults, Book for Children 9 to 12 years old)

Note: Most of the above books are also available in Spanish.

DVDs and Videos

The Catechesis of the Good Shepherd (Sofia's Atria in Rome filmed by photographer Douglas R. Gilbert with text by Sofia Cavaletti).

1: The Atrium of the Youngest Children

2: The Atrium of the Middle Children

3: The Atrium of the Oldest Children

With Silvana Montanaro, M.D., *Discovering the Real Spiritual Life of Children*

The Journal of the Catechesis of the Good Shepherd: Various contributions in the form of articles and letters (1984–2010)

Gobbi, Gianna. *Listening to God with Children*: *The Montessori Method Applied to the Catechesis of Children* (Loveland, OH: Treehaus Communications: 1998).

All of the above are available from the National Association of the Catechesis of the Good Shepherd:
P.O. Box 1084
Oak Park, IL, 60304
phone (708) 524-1210
e-mail cgs@cgusa.org
www.cgsusa.org